Michael Flynn

Muhammad Ali
The People's Champ

Muhammad Ali

The People's Champ

BY AUDREY EDWARDS
WITH GARY WOHL

Boston   Little, Brown and Company   Toronto

COPYRIGHT © 1977 BY AUDREY EDWARDS AND GARY WOHL

ALL RIGHTS RESERVED. NO PART OF THIS BOOK MAY BE REPRODUCED IN ANY FORM OR BY ANY ELECTRONIC OR MECHANICAL MEANS INCLUDING INFORMATION STORAGE AND RETRIEVAL SYSTEMS WITHOUT PERMISSION IN WRITING FROM THE PUBLISHER, EXCEPT BY A REVIEWER WHO MAY QUOTE BRIEF PASSAGES IN A REVIEW.

Second Printing

T 09/77

Library of Congress Cataloging in Publication Data

Edwards, Audrey.
  Muhammad Ali

  SUMMARY: A biography of an Olympic gold medal winner who went on to become heavyweight champion of the world.
  1. Muhammad Ali, 1942– — Juvenile literature.
  2. Boxers — United States — Biography — Juvenile literature. [1. Muhammad Ali, 1942– 2. Boxers]
  I. Wohl, Gary, joint author. II. Title.
  GV1132.M84E39   796.8'3'0924   [B]   [92]   77-4719
  ISBN 0-316-21172-9

792404

*Published simultaneously in Canada
by Little, Brown & Company (Canada) Limited*

PRINTED IN THE UNITED STATES OF AMERICA

*This book is dedicated with love
to every member of our families*

Acknowledgments

This book would not have been possible without the assistance, support, and advice of our editor, Casey Cameron, who cared enough to be demanding, tough, and encouraging.

We would also like to give special thanks to Silvia Koner, the Articles Editor at *Redbook* magazine, who brought us together; our friends Wesley Brown and Fran Ruffin, who reviewed the manuscript and did what only good friends do — gave honest criticism — and Jonathan Goldstein, who so generously gave of his time and legal counsel.

Contents

	Introduction	3
1	The Big, the "Bad," and the Beautiful	7
2	Facing the Bear	19
3	A Capricorn Is Born	36
4	In This Corner, Allah!	61
5	"No Viet Cong Ever Called Me Nigger"	75
6	Out, but Not Down	91
7	The Comeback	104
8	Going Down for the First Time	121
9	After the Fall, the Rise	141
10	The Rumble in the Jungle	155

Muhammad Ali

The People's Champ

Introduction

Aleeeee . . . . . Bomayeeeee! comes the battle cry.

Aleeeee . . . . . Bomayeeeee! comes the roar of the people paying homage to the warrior.

It is October 25, 1974. The place is Zaire, Africa; the time is four in the morning. Here in the hot, smoldering dawn of the African tropics some 60,000 people have gathered to witness the "Fight of the Century" — George Foreman versus Muhammad Ali in a title match for the world heavyweight championship. Foreman the champion. Ali the former champion, back to regain the crown.

It is Ali the people have come to see. It is Ali to whom tribute is being paid. It is Ali who, now on this final testing ground in Zaire, battles not only for a championship title but also for the people and the hope he has come to inspire in them.

Ali is back, though not without a struggle, because he has paid his dues. Ali is back, and the people are rejoicing.

Aleeeee . . . . . Bomayeeeee!

Aleeeee . . . . . Bomayeeeee!

Who is this man, Muhammad Ali, formerly Cassius Clay, who has come to represent both controversy and inspiration?

As Cassius Clay he first came to public attention in 1960 when he won the Gold Medal in boxing at the Rome Olympics. He was only eighteen, but even then he was a brash and cocky guy who would tell you in a minute, "I'm beautiful!" or "I'm the greatest!" or, most likely, both.

He could measure up to both those claims. He stood in at six feet three, with smooth, caramel-colored skin, a perfectly proportioned athlete's body, and a flashing grin that showed pearly teeth. He was a boxer who could take punches without getting his face wasted or bent out of shape like a lot of others in the sport.

He was a boxer who preened in the ring. And danced. Instead of standing flat-footed and slugging it out in the middle of the ring the way most heavyweight fighters do, he was up on his toes — slipping and sliding, bobbing and weaving with the ease and speed and grace of a long-distance runner.

He was a crowd pleaser, often predicting in rhyme, and with startling accuracy, the round in which he would beat an opponent. "They all must fall in the round I call," he would say. He was the loudmouthed kid from Louisville, Kentucky, who carried on with enormous style and wit and made boxing exciting again, a sport worth paying to see.

By the time he was twenty-two, Cassius Clay had turned his sharp tongue and lightning punch into a winning combination that earned him the heavyweight championship crown.

But behind the flamboyant pose and belligerent mouth was also the courage of a disciplined and principled man who would pay the cost of daring to stand by what he believed. A man who would go on to outrage the public when he chose to follow the Black Muslim religion and to honor his Black heritage by changing his name to Muhammad Ali. A man who would defy the law and challenge the system when he refused to be drafted into the U.S. army, believing that it was fighting a racist and immoral war in Viet Nam. A man who would always bravely accept the consequences of his actions.

His outspokenness and his defiant acts took their toll. The "bad-talking" kid from Louisville, who had once been merely amusing, suddenly became despised. He was stripped of his heavyweight championship title and denied the right to box in America for a living. He was forbidden to leave the country. He was threatened with attempts on his life.

However, among certain people — the powerless, the social victims, those seeking to change the existing order — Muhammad Ali came to stand for something. He represented those nobler human instincts that do not compromise values or principles. He came to stand for a higher order based on decency and integrity and honor. He stood as a real champion, one who is never down for the final count.

Ten years elapsed between the time Cassius Clay won the heavyweight championship title to the time Muhammad Ali stepped into the ring to redeem the crown. They were wonderful, bitter, glorious, terrible years. He not only survived them but he emerged victorious, proclaimed a modern-day folk hero, a legend in his own time — still big, still beautiful and still "bad" as ever.

1
The Big, the "Bad," and the Beautiful

This is the story about a man
With iron fists and a beautiful tan
He talks a lot indeed
Of a powerful punch and blinding speed.

The boxing game was slowly dying,
And fight promoters were bitterly crying
For someone, somewhere, to come along
With a better and a different tone.
— *Cassius Clay*

Boxing has always suffered from a split image. It's the only sport that gratifies our animal lust for blood yet at the same time offends our delicate sense of humanity. It's the only sport we've tried to outlaw for its brutality yet will still pay money to see, so as to witness one human being trying to physically destroy another one.

It's the only sport in which an individual can rise to the honor of champion and gain the power of wealth, simply by being the biggest and the strongest in the game, not necessarily the smartest. It's the only sport in which we bet on human beings the way we bet on a racehorse or a rooster in a cockfight.

It's the only sport we both love and hate.

Throughout history, we have always respected human strength. But with boxing we often got the feeling that there wasn't much going on *besides* human strength, and we didn't respect that. Take the kid on the block who has the "baddest" reputation because he's managed to whip everybody: you don't mess with him because you respect his *ability* to whip everybody. But you don't respect *him* if all he can do is work other people over. Boxing has been like that. A sport always half-respected.

Boxing historians claim that the first American boxing champion was a Black slave named Tom Molyneaux. Molyneaux literally fought his way to freedom. His slavemaster used to enter him in fights against the slaves of other masters who would put up betting money and sometimes split part of the take with the slave who won.

Molyneaux won so much, it's reported, that he was finally able to buy his freedom. Still, he was never regarded as more than an ex-slave, and certainly treated with no more real dignity or respect than any other Black man living during slavery.

In fact, it's believed that boxing in America was initially a sport only among slaves — bottom-of-the-totem-pole men who were pitted against each other like animals but often gained some measure of recognition (and even freedom) by being good fighters.

This was also true for many immigrant groups, such as the Irish, the Italians, and the Jews, who were usually at the bottom of the economic heap when they first settled in this country. If they were good fighters, the climb up from the bottom might be quicker. This was true especially if there weren't many other economic opportunities available to them, as was usually the case.

So at first boxing was primarily a pursuit of men who could not make it in the society in acceptable ways. The sport developed a second-class taste to it. It became associated with back-room, back-alley contests in which lusty, beer-drinking, cigar-chomping crowds screamed and hollered and bet on their man as if they were rolling dice in a crap game.

It's not that gentlemen or intellectuals were not attracted to the game of boxing. They were, and have always been, attracted to the sheer physical strength and bodily perfection of the boxer. It's just that you'd never catch gentlemen in a ring, offering up their own bodies for money. They had more dignified ways of making a living. Boxing may have been the manly sport, but it was not a gentlemanly one.

Nor was it thought of as an intellectual's game, or a game for bright men. Of course, there had always been boxers who were smart fighters. They had developed skills and strategies which, in combination with their physical strength, were positively brilliant in the ring. But outside of the ring they were seldom thought of as "smart."

Jack Dempsey, for instance, who was heavyweight champion between 1919 and 1926, was considered a great fighter and even a "gentleman," but people never failed to mention that he ended up being a "mere" saloon keeper after he retired from the ring. Joe Louis, who held the heavyweight title from 1937 to 1949 and defended his crown a record twenty-five times, was considered a great fighter and even a "credit to his race," but people always liked to point out that he wasn't very bright. Floyd Patterson, who was the first fighter to win the heavyweight title twice, first in 1956 and again in 1960, was considered a great fighter and a nice guy who was also "intelligent," but people always noted that he wasn't very interesting.

So, the split image of boxing persisted. It was the one sport in which we glorified the champion and put him down at the same time.

Then Cassius Clay (later he would call himself Muhammad Ali) emerged. A man who would put body and mind together in boxing and elevate the sport from the brutal to the beautiful. A champion who would wear his crown like an arrogant prince — with a strut and a swagger and with style.

Sonny Liston was sitting on the heavyweight throne when Cassius Clay came to public prominence in the early nineteen-sixties. Liston had defeated "nice guy" Floyd Patterson twice, both times in the first round, to win the heavyweight crown. Liston was rated by boxing experts as "invincible." It seemed he would wear the championship crown for as long as he wanted.

However, with Liston the crown had become a little tarnished. He brought to it a prison record stretching back to his teenage years. It wasn't that Liston was the first or the only boxing champion to have done time in prison, for in boxing's early days many fighters had criminal records. But he was viewed as so big and so Black and so mean that he loomed as a public enemy instead of a world champion.

He was reported even to have had mob connections, which did nothing to help his reputation or the image of boxing. As time wore on, the excitement of watching him easily demolish opponents in the ring soon began to fade. The public grew bored, sportswriters grew blasé, and fight promoters went broke. Boxing seemed on its way out as a sport, with nothing more to recommend it than an ex-con, heavyweight champion who would probably be around forever.

It took Cassius Clay, a loudmouthed, arrogant kid from Louisville, Kentucky, to turn the game around. He not only injected it with fresh blood, but also transformed it into a truly exciting sport, with an appeal that would cut across class and color and nationality.

From the very beginning, Cassius Clay was out to win big in boxing — without getting his face wasted. "Games is only for a little while," he said, "but your face is forever." This was an attitude that seemed to shape his whole approach to the sport: make a lot of money, have a little fun, and, above all, stay pretty.

While other fighters who got their faces and minds destroyed eventually went punch drunk, Cassius intended to keep his body and his brain intact. And he was the only modern fighter who knew how to use his intelligence both in and out of the ring to maximum effect.

He knew that boxing is a sport in which everything rides on the performance of one man. So he became a performer, hustling people with a calculated sales pitch designed to shock his public yet still make them turn out for his fights.

Fighting since he was twelve years old, Cassius would mouth off to anyone who would listen about what he was going to do to another kid in the ring. "I'm the greatest!" became his standard rap. For Cassius recognized the power of a gimmick. People would invariably flock to Cassius's fights in the hopes of seeing his opponent shut his mouth. As far as Cassius was concerned, it didn't matter why they came, only that they came. For he was born a showman as much as a boxer, with a tremendous ego. From childhood he loved the sound and the fury of a crowd, whether cheering him on to victory or screaming for his destruction.

Cassius also knew enough about human nature to realize that he could hope to defeat an opponent in the ring by first "messing with his mind" out of the ring. When heavyweight champion Floyd Patterson showed up at the 1960 Rome Olympics to watch Cassius fight, Cassius spotted him and screamed, "Floyd Patterson! Someday I'm going to whip you! I'm the greatest!" Patterson just smiled, but he was already being set up. Cassius was a master at wearing his opponent down mentally and then finishing him off in the ring.

Sportswriters began to suspect that this cocky kid whom they dubbed "The Louisville Lip" might actually have a clever mind behind his brazen mouth. At last, something different and interesting was happening in boxing. Even if you didn't like the kid, you couldn't help noticing him. And as far as Cassius was concerned, that was the whole point.

After winning the Gold Medal at the Olympics, Cassius worked on improving his outrageous antics. He took to writing bold poetry that predicted the round in which he would knock out an opponent.

"When you come to the fight/ Don't block the halls/ And don't block the door/ For y'all may go home/ After round four," he wrote in 1962 about his upcoming fight with Archie Moore, a former light heavyweight champion, who had recently moved into the heavyweight division.

Probably the person with the greatest impact on the development of Cassius's flamboyant style was Gorgeous George. George was, like Cassius, a braggart. He was a professional wrestler, but he spent most of his time strutting around in purple tights and golden bleached curls, swirling a cape behind him and proclaiming in gory detail how he was going to demolish his next opponent. When he and Cassius appeared on a radio show together in 1961, each to discuss an upcoming fight, the announcer asked Gorgeous George how he thought his fight would go.

"I'm gonna kill him!" George bellowed, jumping up and down and pounding the table with his huge hand. "I'm gonna kill him! They shouldn't even bother to hold the match. It's a waste of my time. He's a dead man!"

Cassius was impressed, and ended up going to the match to see Gorgeous George in action for himself. He wasn't disappointed. George stomped and shrieked, groaned and grunted, and generally raged ferociously. Cassius sat spellbound.

"Ain't he sumptin'?" he kept saying. "Ain't he sumptin'!"

With Gorgeous George as his inspiration, Cassius pushed his own act to the limit. He began showing up in unlikely places, proclaiming "I'm the greatest!" "I'm the prettiest fighter that ever lived!" "I'm gonna be champion!" "I'm too pretty to get beat!"

He would show up at other boxing matches, sit ringside, and shout to the winner, "Hey, chump! I can beat you!" At an Archie Moore fight, he screamed, "Hey, Moore, you ain't nothing but an old man! Wait till I get you in the ring!"

He showed up at the Bitter End nightclub in Greenwich Village, New York, one night to read his latest poem in a poetry contest. Before the contest was over, he announced that he was the winner. "It's no contest!" he shouted. "I'm the winner 'cause I'm the greatest!"

He went on Johnny Carson's "Tonight Show" to recite his shortest poem: "Wheeeee! Me!"

The kid from Louisville was making an impression, all right.

"You love me and you hate me 'cause I talk too loud and too much," he would shout at the crowds that soon rushed to see his fights. "I'm the greatest, the fastest, the prettiest,

The "Louisville Lip" sounds off at a press conference.

the danciest heavyweight boxer in the world, and you know it!"

He was right. At least, he was right about people loving and hating him. People hated his mouth but loved the idea of being on hand for his fights in case his opponent closed it.

He was also right about being a pretty fighter. Cassius managed to come out of every fight unscarred, his face still flawless, and his body looking as though it hadn't even perspired.

His wide, high-cheekboned face was accentuated by deep-set black eyes and heavy brows. His full, sensual mouth could flash a boyishly charming grin one minute, and an innocently sexy smile the next. His 6'3" frame had been light when he first started boxing professionally, but by the early sixties he had filled out to a heavy-muscled, well-proportioned build, averaging around 220 pounds. Physically, Cassius was the first boxer to gain wide appeal among both men and women — men being attracted to the "he-man" image of his superior physique, women being attracted to the sexuality he suggested.

The public acknowledged that Cassius was indeed a good-looking fighter. But they knew he wasn't the greatest yet. In the first place, his fighting style seemed almost suicidal for a heavyweight boxer. He carried his hands too low, he pulled back too often, exposing both his face and body to his opponent, and he moved on his toes, dancing back and forth in constant motion, sometimes at dizzying speeds that seemed likely to throw him off balance. Secondly, Cassius didn't appear to be a particularly powerful puncher.

Still, all those people who were flocking to Cassius's fights in the hopes of seeing him get his mouth shut left disappointed. Cassius had fought 19 professional fights by the time he was twenty-one and had won all of them, 15 by knockouts. He was evidently doing something right in the ring.

What he was doing was moving with lightning speed — both on his feet and with his punches. He could get away with pulling back, carrying his hands low, and moving on his toes, because he was the fastest thing with two feet and two hands that had ever stepped into a boxing ring. He had enormous energy that allowed him to maintain his speed while his opponents tired out from trying to catch him. And if his punches weren't always devastating in their strength (although they could be), they worked because they were usually unexpected by his opponent, coming with dazzling speed, seemingly out of nowhere.

Yet, Cassius made boxing look almost effortless. He glided in the ring, fancy two-stepping left and right, shuffling on his toes, moving with the grace and ease of a nimble dancer. He made boxing rhythmical. He made it an art. He gave it some class. "Float like a butterfly, sting like a bee!" became the battle chant that described his style and his power in the ring.

By the time he reached twenty-one, Cassius Clay was the most exciting sports figure on the American scene. His boasting alone drew record crowds to his fights. He was the fighter you loved to hate. He was the crowd pleaser and the show-stopping entertainer who was just as thrilling to watch out of the ring as in it.

At age twenty-one, Cassius announced that he was ready to take on Sonny Liston for the world heavyweight championship title match. The public went wild. "The Louisville Lip" in a fight against "Sonny The Terrible"? It would be a fight to end all fights. It was a fight promoter's dream. Cassius himself predicted a $100 million gate if the fight was shown internationally by satellite hookup. "I'm very big in those foreign countries," he declared. "They love me over there."

Of course, nobody was betting on Cassius to win. The kid was good, but not that good, and against Sonny, the invincible, he didn't stand a chance. Or did he?

2
Facing the Bear

Bet on Sonny,
Lose your money.
Float like a butterfly,
Sting like a bee,
Bet your money,
Bet on me.
— *Cassius Clay*

The bus was named Big Red, and it came barreling through the cold, foggy night at two in the morning. As it approached the outskirts of Denver, Colorado, and slowed down, the bright, bold lettering on both sides of the bus became clearly visible. Across one side was the message, "The World's Most Colorful Fighter," and underneath was the name Cassius Clay. Across the other side was a prediction: "Sonny Liston is great, but he'll fall in eight."

The bus stopped at a gas station and the driver asked directions to Sonny Liston's house. Then the bus driver called some of the city newspapers with a hot story.

"Listen," he said, "Cassius Clay just drove into Denver. He's at Sonny Liston's house and he's getting ready to break in!"

The bus, continuing on its journey, was now cruising through a fashionable section of town. In the distance came the sound of police sirens: *Ahhhhh! Ahhhhh!* They were getting closer.

The bus pulled up in front of a house. Someone got out, ran up to the door, and started banging on it and shouting:

"Hey! Liston! Come on out! You hear me? Get your ugly self out here!"

The bus horn was blaring: Honk! Honk! And the people in the bus were shouting: *"Hey! Liston!* Get out here!"

The whole neighborhood woke up.

Liston stuck his head out of the window, and couldn't believe his eyes. Parked in his yard was a bus painted orange, yellow, green, blue, but mostly red. Inside was Cassius Clay, his brother Rudolph, and his friends Ronnie King and Clay Tyson. The man banging on Liston's door was Howard Bingham, Cassius's photographer. The people in the bus were still shouting and pressing on the horn. *"Oink! Oink!"* they screamed.

Liston let out a growl that sounded like a lion's roar. *"Hey!* Get out of my yard!" Then he came running out of his house, dressed in polka-dot pajamas, and waving an iron poker from his fireplace. "Get the hell outa here!" he raged.

Cassius locked the bus door just before Liston smashed one of the windows with the poker and started banging on the others.

Suddenly there was the blinding flash of car headlights. A police car was screeching to a halt in front of Liston's house. Two policemen and a police dog jumped out, and as the policemen were pulling Liston back to his house, one of them saw and recognized Cassius. "Boy, if you're not out of this town in the next hour, you're going to jail!" he yelled.

Cassius started the bus motor, but as he was pulling out he screamed to Liston, "You ugly *bear!* The police and those dogs saved you! You no champ! You a *chump!* You gonna fall in eight 'cause I'm the greatest! I'm the greatest! I'm the *greatest!*" he kept shouting.

By now newspapermen were beginning to arrive. But Cassius stepped on the gas, and in a cloud of smoke the bus went rolling off into the night.

The next day a story appeared in all the Denver newspapers saying that Cassius had raided Sonny Liston's house at two in the morning, and that it had taken ten policemen and six police dogs to break up the fight between Cassius and Liston and to run Cassius out of town! Cassius liked the exaggeration. He knew that people would now be even more anxious to see him fight Liston. And he remembered the look on Liston's face the night before — angry and also a little scared.

It had taken Cassius almost a year to convince fight promoters that he should be given a shot at the championship title in a fight with Liston. It was a year of stalking and hounding and teasing Liston every chance he got.

Liston first became world heavyweight champion in 1962 after beating Floyd Patterson in the first two minutes of the first round. Right on the spot, Cassius climbed into the ring after Liston won the fight and challenged him to a fight. Cassius was only twenty years old at the time. He would have to wait a while longer for his chance to take a crack at the world championship. But he was confident of his ability to beat Liston. Besides, he knew that no matter how great he said he was, people wouldn't really believe it unless he proved he could win against the invincible Sonny Liston.

While Liston was training for his second fight with Patterson in Las Vegas, Cassius decided to pay him a visit. He wanted to watch Liston train, and also to bug him a little.

But one night while he was in Las Vegas, Cassius discovered Liston could play a few mean tricks of his own.

Liston was in one of the casinos gambling, when one of his trainers suggested to Cassius that he go over to the table and spend some money too. Cassius went over gladly.

"But I'm not gonna spend any money," he told the trainer. "I'm gonna run him outa the casino!" As Cassius approached the table, he saw that Liston was deep in a dice game. Cassius started shouting at him.

"Come on, you ugly bear! Let's get it on! Come *on!*"

Liston didn't bother to look up.

Cassius kept screaming. "I'll whip you right now!" he said. "Floyd Patterson is a nobody. You'll knock out Patterson, but I'm the real champ. I'm too fast for you, and you *know* it! Put up your money, Sonny! If you think you can whip me!"

Liston still didn't look up. But everyone else in the

room had stopped playing. They started walking over to Liston's table to see what was happening. The room grew quiet. Cassius knew he had the total attention of the crowd and he loved it. He walked right up to Liston for a showdown.

"I want you out of town by sunup tomorrow," he said. "Las Vegas ain't big enough for both of us."

Suddenly, Liston reached in his coat pocket and pulled out a long, black pistol. He aimed it straight at Cassius's head and fired! *Bang! Bang!*

Cassius ducked. *Bang! Bang!* Liston fired again, still aiming at Cassius. Cassius leaped over a blackjack table, then a dice table, knocking chips and cards all over the floor. He was ducking and dodging, and Liston was still firing. *Bang! Bang! Bang!*

Cassius ran out of the casino onto the street and straight back to his hotel room. He locked the door and then threw himself across the bed, sweating and panting and shaking. "Whew!" he said to himself. "Maybe I should leave Liston alone. I'm only *acting* crazy when I tease him, but he might be crazy for *real!*"

Later Cassius learned that Liston's trainer, the man who had suggested that Cassius go gamble with Liston, had told Liston that Cassius was coming. He had given Liston the gun to fire, but it was filled with blanks! And both Liston and his trainer broke out laughing when they saw Cassius running out of the casino like a scared rabbit. The joke was on him for a change!

Cassius had to laugh himself. And yet he didn't like the

idea of being on the other end of a joke. Especially when it was played on him by the man he was determined to beat.

Sonny Liston gained the reputation of being unbeatable after he knocked out Floyd Patterson in two fights, both times within the first two minutes of the first round. Looking at Liston, it wasn't hard to see how he'd managed to do that. He stood 6'1", with a massive, bull-like head and a thick, powerful body that looked as though it had the strength of a brick wall.

The knuckles on his huge hands measured 14 inches across, and early in life Liston had decided his fists were his best friends. But his fists also got him into trouble.

Born in a small town in Arkansas, Charles Liston came from a very poor, sharecropping family. In addition to Liston's own twelve brothers and sisters, his father had twelve children from another marriage, making a total of twenty-five children in the family. They all wore hand-me-down clothing, and spent more time helping to work the farm than in school. "If they're old enough to eat, they're old enough to work," Liston's father would say about his children. He was a stern and cruel man, and Liston remembered being yelled at and beaten almost every day.

When Liston was thirteen, he ran away from home to St. Louis, Missouri, to join his mother, who left the family to go to work in the city. But the first year he was in St. Louis he got arrested, reportedly for assault. He was released to the custody of his mother.

By the time he was sixteen, Liston had fallen in with a

street gang who would hold robberies just for kicks. By 1950, when he was only eighteen, he had been arrested for six muggings! He was already a 200-pounder, and was unbelievably strong. Once he picked up the front end of a Ford car just because somebody said he couldn't do it!

Liston was quick with his fists and known to have an equally quick temper. In 1950 a St. Louis gas station was robbed and two people were beaten up. Liston was charged with the crime, found guilty and sentenced to two consecutive five-year sentences in the Missouri State Penitentiary. He was paroled in 1952.

Liston started boxing while he was in prison. A policeman once said that if it hadn't been for boxing Liston probably would have continued to lead a life of crime, and ended up dead with a bullet in his back.

Still, even though Liston turned "legitimate" when he started boxing professionally, people continued to think of him as an ex-con. And his personality didn't do much to help that image. He was a cold and brooding man whose face seemed to bear only two expressions: a hostile stare or a growling snarl. Because he felt that life had given him a raw deal, he was suspicious of most people and trusted practically no one.

In 1956 Liston was accused of beating up a policeman after a party he and his wife had attended. Although Liston's version of what happened differed from the policeman's, he was convicted and sentenced to nine months in jail. Again he was paroled, after serving seven months.

Back in the ring, by 1962 Liston had won thirty-four

fights and lost only one. And twenty-three of his wins had been by knockouts! But in the early sixties he was also reported to have racketeer connections. In fact, it was charged that the mob controlled him. Liston even had to testify before a Senate commission that was investigating organized crime's control of boxing. He said that, as far as he knew, no racketeers "owned a piece of" him.

Given his grim past, the public dreaded the thought of a man like Liston becoming world heavyweight champion. He was often described as a cop beater, an ex-con and an evil brute. One sportswriter even called him the King Kong of boxing after he won the championship.

When Liston defeated Floyd Patterson in Chicago in 1962, most of the more than 18,000 people in the audience booed and jeered. Sonny Liston was crowned champion — the odds had been on him to win — but as one writer said, he was "the champ nobody wanted." It was true.

Liston had paid his debt to society by serving a prison sentence, and promised to wear the crown with dignity. But he was still regarded as a criminal by most people. And no one wanted a criminal for a champion. The only problem was, there didn't seem to be anyone else around who would stand a chance of taking the crown away from him. Not Floyd Patterson, not the three other men Liston beat after defeating Patterson, and certainly not the loudmouthed kid from Louisville who was next in line for a shot at the title.

The Cassius Clay–Sonny Liston fight deal was finally signed in November of 1963. The fight would be held the next year in February in Miami Beach, Florida. After the contract had been signed, Cassius told reporters, very simply, that he wasn't afraid of Liston.

"He's an old man," Cassius said. (Liston was thirty-two.) "I'll give him talking lessons and boxing lessons, and what he needs most, which is falling down lessons!"

But the odds were 7–1 against Cassius to win. And he had had trouble even getting a state to allow the match to be held in the first place. (Each state has a boxing commission which decides whether or not a fight can take place in that state.)

A California boxing investigator stated, "The proposed Cassius Clay–Sonny Liston heavyweight title fight is a dangerous mismatch which could result in grave injury to the young challenger. Besides," he continued, "not one former heavyweight champion thinks Clay is ready for Liston."

He was right about that. Former heavyweight champion Rocky Marciano, discussing the fight, said " 'The Lip' should see a good psychiatrist. He's too inexperienced to be taking on a brute like Liston."

Ex-champ Joe Louis said, quite bluntly, "He's got to be kidding."

Other people joked about the fight. "I'm betting on Clay — to live!" said one comedian. Another comedian, Jackie Gleason, said, "Clay should last about eighteen seconds, and that includes the three seconds he brings with him!" (The three men who are in the ring corner with a boxer during a fight are known as "seconds.")

Even the usually close-mouthed Sonny Liston himself had a few choice words to say about the fight. "That fag won't last a round," he predicted. "And if he does make it to the fight, I'll probably be locked up for murder!"

Of course, most people were excited about the prospect of a Clay-Liston match because they saw a chance for the Louisville Lip's mouth to be shut for once and probably forever. Since Liston was not exactly beloved by the public, people were looking forward to the fight, not so much to see Liston win, but to see Cassius *lose*. Cassius was the main attraction, and he knew it.

And because he knew it, he demanded that he get the money he wanted for the fight. He had even gone on television in Louisville a few months before the fight contract was signed to threaten that the fight would be called off if he didn't get his purse.

"There will be no fight between Liston and I until the money is right," he said. "He [Liston] either meets my price or he can dance elsewhere for peanuts. I don't need Sonny Liston, he needs *me*. I'm the hottest attraction to come along since talking pictures."

Cassius finally got his price, nearly half a million dollars! The fight was scheduled for February 25, 1964, in Miami Beach's Convention Hall. The match was expected to bring in eight million dollars! — a figure unheard of in the history of boxing. Cassius not only talked a good game, but he talked big money!

The day of a boxing match is always the day of the weigh-in ceremony — usually a dignified, but unexciting, affair during which time the boxers are weighed, measured, examined by doctors, and interviewed by reporters.

On the morning of the fight, Cassius entered the weigh-in room first, wearing a blue denim work jacket with the words "Bear Hunting" written in red across the back. Accompanying him were Sugar Ray Robinson, the good-looking, ex-light heavyweight champion, and Drew "Bundini" Brown, Cassius's friend and sidekick.

Cassius spotted the reporters and ran up to them yelling, "You can tell Sonny I'm here with Sugar Ray. The two prettiest dancers in the world are *here!*" he shouted.

Then he turned to Bundini, and the two of them chanted their battle cry as loud as they could: *"Float like a butterfly! Sting like a bee! Float like a butterfly! Sting like a bee!"*

Cassius took off his jacket and pants and went up on the platform in his boxing trunks to be weighed. He insisted that Sugar Ray and Bundini follow him. A few minutes later Liston entered the room, followed by a crowd of supporters and roaring applause. Suddenly it seemed as though Liston were the champion everybody *did* want!

Liston stepped on the scale first, but as he stepped off and reached for his robe, Cassius seemed to go crazy.

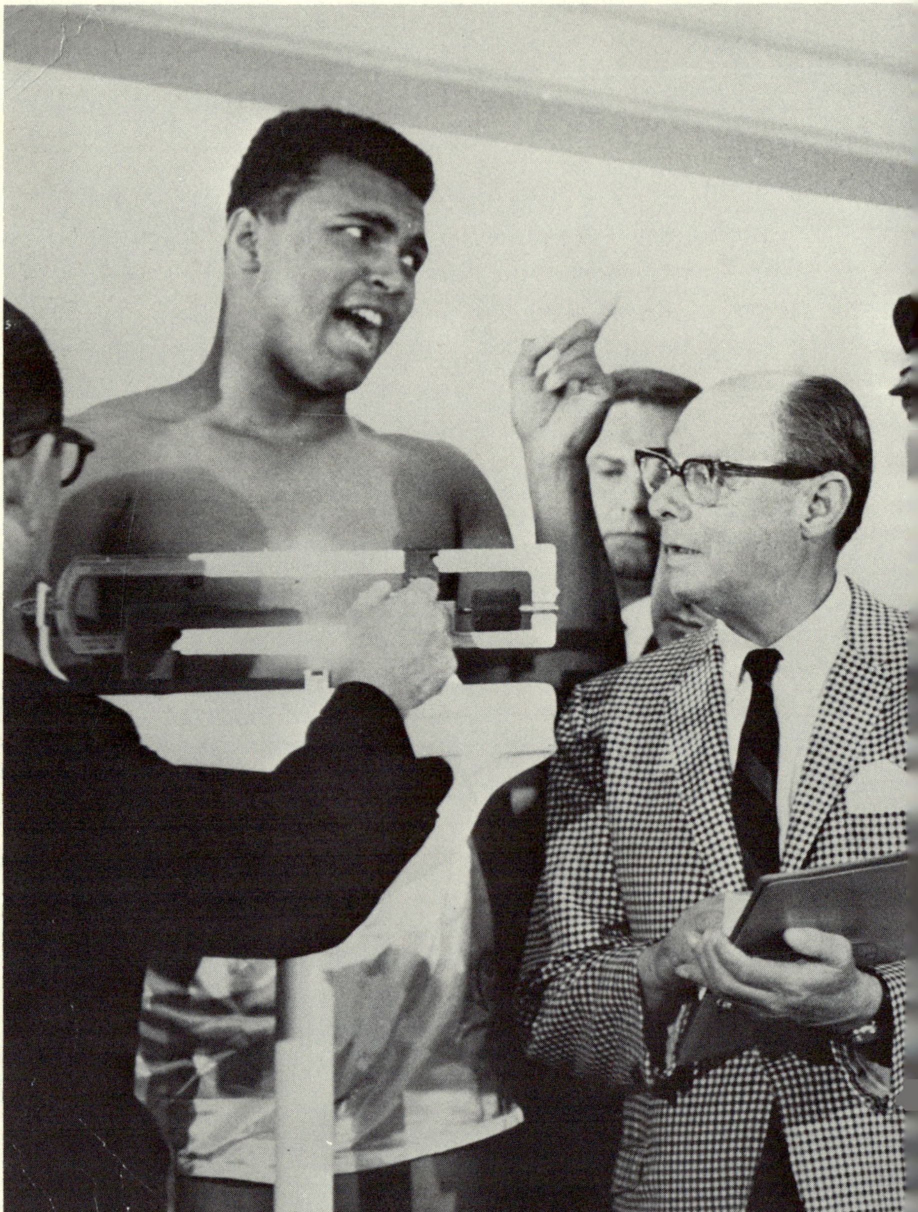

Cassius on stage at the weigh-in for his heavyweight title fight against Sonny Liston in Miami. Cassius is giving Liston some "lip," while Liston gives him the "stare." (CAMERA 5, KEN REGAN)

"Hey, sucker! You're a chump!" Cassius screamed, jumping toward Liston. "You've been tricked!"

Liston smiled wickedly, but Cassius went on.

"You're too ugly!" he said. "You're a bear! I'm going to whip you so *baaad*. You're a chump, a chump, a chump...!"

Cassius was screaming at the top of his lungs. His face was twisted. He was jumping up and down, waving his arms like a wild man and reaching for Liston as though he was going to wipe him out on the spot. Sugar Ray and Bundini were holding him back.

The crowd of reporters was horrified. "Clay's gone stark, raving mad!" they said to each other. "He's so afraid of Liston that he's become hysterical."

Even the doctor who examined Cassius was astonished. Cassius's normal pulse rate of 54 had shot up to 120! "Clay is nervous and scared to death, and he's burning up a lot of energy," the doctor stated. It was frightening.

It was also an act. Cassius had staged the whole ranting and raving routine at the weigh-in on purpose, and for one purpose: to scare *Liston* to death. An hour after the weigh-in Cassius's pulse rate was back to normal. Again the doctors were amazed. But Liston *was* running scared, no doubt wondering if later that night he might, indeed, be getting into the ring with a madman!

Cassius had predicted that he would beat Liston by the eighth round, but recently his predictions had not been hitting the mark. Although he had defeated ex-champion Archie Moore "in four," the way he predicted when he fought him in November of 1962, he had gone the whole fight length with Doug Jones, a contender he said would fall in six. So people were not only betting on Cassius to lose, but were paying no attention at all to his prediction.

On the night of February 25, 1964, over 8,000 people were jammed into Convention Hall to see what was being called "The Greatest Grudge Fight in History" — the Sonny Liston–Cassius Clay world heavyweight championship match. Another 860,000 people had paid to watch the fight over closed-circuit television in movie houses around the country.

The referee gave prefight instructions to Cassius and Liston while the two men stood in the ring, staring at each other. Cassius was finally face to face with "The Bear."

The bell rang for round one. Liston moved in quickly for the kill. He threw the first punch, a long, left jab that missed by a foot. Cassius was on his toes moving backward and from side to side. Liston threw another punch. Missed again. Cassius was doing his shuffle, and Liston was trying to catch him.

The second round was like the first. Cassius dancing, and Liston missing. Liston had Cassius cornered for a moment, but Cassius slipped away, bobbing and weaving around the ring.

During the third round Cassius started throwing some punches of his own. He stopped dancing and hit Liston with a jab, a right uppercut and a left hook combination. And just before the bell rang, ending the round, Cassius bombarded him with a series of blows. One of them cut a deep gash under Liston's left eye.

The crowd began to murmur. This fight wasn't turning out the way they had expected at all!

During round four Liston's fighting performance got worse. Especially since Cassius was now whispering to him as he tried to get in a punch. "I'm the greatest! I'm the greatest!" Cassius kept saying. Liston was starting to believe him!

But before the bell sounded for round five, Cassius got something in his eyes that was blinding him. "I can't see! I can't see!" he screamed to his trainer, Angelo Dundee. "Cut the gloves off. Take them off!" Cassius wanted to end the fight! He thought the fight had been fixed, that someone had put something in his eyes to blind him so he would lose. His trainer, however, would not let Cassius stop the fight.

"Are you crazy?" he said to Cassius. "You're winning! Get back out there!"

Cassius managed to get through round five, although he could barely see. It turned out that the medication which had been put on Liston's cut eye had gotten on his gloves, which meant when he hit Cassius, some of it went in his eyes.

By round six, Cassius's vision had cleared. He came out swinging in every direction at Liston. He was still convinced that Liston had tried to fix the fight.

Liston tried to back away from Cassius's blows, but Cassius kept coming. He punched and pounded at Liston until blood covered his entire face. Liston looked weak. When the bell rang ending the round, Cassius could feel that victory was near.

The bell rang for round seven. Something was wrong. Liston wasn't getting up. It took a few minutes for the crowd to realize what had happened, and Cassius recognized it first. By not getting up, Liston was admitting defeat! That meant the fight was over. And that meant Cassius was the new world heavyweight champion in boxing!

"I told you! I told you! — I'm the greatest!" Cassius suddenly cried to the crowd as he ran around the ring with his arms held up high in victory. The crowd was stunned. This young, twenty-two-year-old loudmouthed kid had just beaten Sonny Liston, the unbeatable!

"Who's the greatest?" Cassius asked the reporters who were swamping him with questions during a press conference the next day. No one answered.

"Who's the greatest?" Cassius asked again. Still no answer.

"*Who's the greatest?*" he asked for the last time.

"*You* are," the reporters mumbled.

"Well, *all right!*" Cassius shouted triumphantly. "The Greatest" was now ready to answer any questions from the press.

3
A Capricorn Is Born

It all started twenty years past,
The greatest of them was born at last.
The very first words from his Louisville lips,
"I'm pretty as a picture, and there's no one I can't whip."
— *Cassius Clay*

The startled reporters who were crammed into Cassius's dressing room after the fight were throwing out questions with the speed of shotgun blasts.

"How'd ya do it, kid?" several of them kept asking, still unable to comprehend that he had just beaten Sonny Liston.

"Do you think it was just luck . . . ?"

"Would you get in the ring with Liston again?"

"Some people say Liston had a bad shoulder, and wasn't up to par. . . ."

Cassius, with a grin, answered the questions almost as quickly as they were being asked. No, he said, he knew his win over Liston hadn't been just luck. He had been preparing for this day nearly all of his life — almost as far back as January 17, 1942, the day Mrs. Odessa Clay gave birth to a six-pound, seven-ounce baby boy in Louisville's General Hospital.

It was a difficult birth. The baby's head was so big that it seemed to take forever to come out. The doctors finally had to pull it out with forceps.

A few hours after the birth a nurse brought the baby in to Mrs. Clay. He was a quiet, peaceful child who lay cuddled in Mrs. Clay's arms. She sensed something was wrong. This baby was mighty quiet — too quiet. The new mother happened to glance at the name tag on the baby's arm and saw that it said "Brown," not "Clay."

"Where's my child?" Mrs. Clay suddenly cried. "This is not my child! Look," she said to the nurse, "this baby's name is Brown!"

"Oh, my goodness!" exclaimed the nurse. She took the baby away, and a few minutes later returned with another one. He was screaming and hollering and making so much noise that Mrs. Clay jumped when she took him in her arms. "Now, *this* is my child!" she said with a knowing smile.

The baby was named Cassius Marcellus Clay, after his father, who in turn had been named for a famous Kentucky statesman and abolitionist.

Cassius, Jr., was a late Capricorn, born on the cusp with Aquarius, a combination that usually provides for a forceful and determined nature. Capricorns born on the date of January 17 are also said to possess good common sense. But they tend to be high-strung, and since they are very ambitious, they can become quite angry if anything gets in the way of their progress.

At the age of ten months Cassius started to talk. When

he was about a year old, Cassius became angry at his mother, who was spanking him, and reached up and accidentally hit her in the mouth with his little fist. The punch loosened one of her teeth. Already, by age one, Cassius was beginning to make his mark as a fighter!

The Clay family lived in the West End area of Louisville, one of the three Black sections in the city. It wasn't as nice as the best Black section, called the California Area. But it was much better than the worst section, known as the East End, or "Snake Town."

Cassius's father, who worked as a sign painter, wasn't making much money when Cassius was first born, but over the years his reputation grew, and so did his income. Cassius Clay, Sr., is still a dapper man who likes to dress in fancy clothes and eye pretty ladies when he steps out. He's also quite a talker, so talking came naturally for Cassius, Jr.

Odessa Clay, a pretty and plump, cheerful woman, gave birth to another son two years after Cassius was born. He was named Rudolph Valentino Clay, after the dashing silent-movie star. He and Cassius were inseparable. Often, if Rudy was about to be spanked by his mother, Cassius would come in and rescue him. "Don't you hit my baby," he would shout.

At school Cassius wasn't a very good student. He would rather spend time doing crazy things to get attention than studying the books. He learned early that everybody likes (or at least pays attention to) people who are different.

"Hey, look at Cassius," kids on the school bus used to say

almost everyday. Instead of riding the bus, Cassius would run beside it, trying to beat it to school!

Cassius was twelve when an incident happened that would determine the course of his life. He had just received a brand new bicycle for his birthday, and was riding around town with his best buddy, Johnny Willis. It started raining and the boys wanted to go somewhere for cover.

"I got an idea," said Johnny. "The big home show over at Columbia Auditorium has started, and there's free hot dogs and popcorn and candy. Whatya say we go on over?"

"Free popcorn? Sure!" said Cassius, who was ready to do about anything to get out of the rain. This would also be a good opportunity to show off his new Schwinn bike with its red lights, chrome trim, and spotlight in the front, since the show drew a big crowd every year.

The auditorium was a large recreational center that had a gym in the basement. Cassius and Johnny were so busy stuffing themselves with hot dogs and popcorn that they forgot all about the time.

"Hey, I better get on home before my father starts having a fit," Cassius said when he realized it was late.

"Okay," said Johnny. "Let's go."

But when the boys got outside, Cassius's bike was gone! "Where's my bike?" he cried. "Oh, no! Don't tell me someone's done stole my new bike. My dad's gonna kill me!"

Cassius was crying, and ran back in to the auditorium to see if anybody knew who had taken the bike.

"There's a policeman downstairs in the gym," somebody

told him. "You'd better go down and tell him what happened."

Cassius ran downstairs and headed straight for the tall, thin white policeman named Joe Martin. Cassius knew the policeman, who managed the gym and trained boxers during his spare time.

"Mr. Martin, Mr. Martin!" Cassius shouted, "My bike is gone. Somebody took my bike. I looked all over and it's gone! It's *gone!*"

"All right, now just take it easy," said Martin. "You will have to give me a report." Martin started writing down the information about the stolen bike, and then noticed that Cassius had stopped talking. He looked up and saw Cassius staring intently at a young boxer, shadowboxing in a corner of the gym. There were about ten other boxers in the gym. Some were in the rings, others were hitting the speed bag, and some were jumping rope. But Cassius kept looking at the skinny kid shadowboxing. "Wow, look at him!" Cassius almost whispered. "He's throwing punches so fast my eyes can't even follow them." Then Cassius suddenly blurted, "Hey, I can do that!" He jumped up on his toes and moved from side to side boxing the air.

"I wanna learn how to box so I can find the chump who stole my bike and beat him up good," he said to Martin.

"First things first," replied Martin, who told Cassius he had to finish filling out the report on the stolen bicycle. Later, as Cassius was ready to leave the gym, Martin said, "Look, we got boxing every night Monday through Friday, from six to eight. Here's an application if you want to join the gym."

Cassius took the form and put it in his pocket. He almost started to cry again when he remembered that he was going home without his new bicycle. He dreaded having to face his father.

"Where you been?" his father demanded to know, when Cassius came in the door. "And where's your bike?"

Cassius told his father what happened. "What!" cried his father. "You mean to tell me I spend my hard-earned money to buy you a bike and you can't even keep it? Boy, I oughta whip you!" But Mr. Clay could see that his son felt worse than he did about losing the bike, and had already been punished enough.

"All right, son," he sighed. "You go on up to bed now."

As Cassius went into his room he was thinking that if he ever got hold of the person who took his bicycle he would probably try to kill him.

The next Saturday night Cassius was home, watching TV. An amateur boxing show called "Tomorrow's Champions" came on, and Cassius suddenly recognized the face of the policeman Joe Martin he had spoken to the week before. Martin was in a ring corner with one of the boxers.

"Bird," Cassius said nudging his mother. (Cassius always called his mother "Bird" because he thought her round, golden face and reddish-brown curls were "pretty as a bird.") "That's the man I told about the bicycle. He wants me to come and box."

Cassius knew that the Black boxers training over at the Grace Community Center in the East End section were much better fighters than Martin's. The manager there, Fred Stoner, was teaching his fighters fancy footwork and better rhythm strategies.

Martin wouldn't permit his fighters to box any of the East End boys. He didn't even want them near Fred Stoner's gym. But Cassius started sneaking over anyway, without telling Martin, since he still wanted to get his four dollars every week for going on TV.

The work at Stoner's gym was much rougher. Each fighter had to do one hundred push-ups and one hundred knee bends every day. Stoner would have the boys develop such punches as the left jab and right cross by practicing the same punch over and over at least 200 times. If the fighters got tired and stopped, he would make them start all over again. Jab, jab, jab . . . 200 times. Pretty soon, Cassius could do 200 jabs and right crosses without even feeling it.

He continued to appear on television. One hot Saturday morning, when he was about thirteen, he met, in front of a swimming pool, a skinny boy who turned out to be his opponent on the show that night. But later that evening, when the two were weighing in, officials said the boy was too skinny to fight Cassius. Cassius was outraged. Because of this, he couldn't fight that night and would lose his four dollars.

The boy's name was Jimmy Ellis. Years later he and Cassius would box each other in two amateur matches.

"Hey, Cash," the kids cried. "You gonna take that? You gonna let him talk to you like that, Cash?"

Cassius knew the time had come. His reputation was on the line. If he didn't whip Corky, he would never be considered the real king. He challenged Corky right then to a boxing match at the gym.

"I done told you, boxing's a sissy sport, man!" Corky replied. "I ain't got time for no sissy fighting."

"Well, man, if it's so sissy, it oughta be easy," Cassius said.

The kids in the yard agreed. "Hey, Corky, you ain't afraid of no sissy fight, are you?" they said, laughing.

"Naw, man, I ain't afraid," Corky said, looking straight at Cassius. "Come on, let's go."

Cassius knew he didn't stand a chance fighting Corky on the street, where there were no rules or regulations or referee. But it would be a different game in the ring — his game.

The whole schoolyard crowd followed Cassius and Corky over to the gym. "Corky'll shut his big mouth," they were saying. "Cash might be a good fighter, but his mouth is too big, and Corky's gonna break his spine."

The match was set to last three rounds. When the bell rang, Corky rushed out and took a big swipe at Cassius and missed. Cassius was already beginning to perfect his style of moving fast and leaning back.

By the middle of the second round, Corky was worn out, and Cassius had blackened his eye. "Hell, no!" Corky suddenly yelled, throwing up his hands. "This ain't fair!"

He staggered out of the ring and hurried into the dressing room to get his clothes. He had quit and was admitting defeat!

The kids from Central High jumped and hollered and lifted Cassius on their shoulders. " 'The King' is dead!" they shouted. "We all free now!" Carrying Cassius high, they marched out into the street. He was the new king — king of the gym, king of Central High and now king of the streets. And he would soon be on his way to becoming boxing king of the world.

In 1959 Cassius won the National Golden Gloves championship in boxing and the national boxing title in the Amateur Athletic Union's (AAU) competition. Winning both these championships made him eligible to participate in the summer Olympics, which were being held in Rome the next year.

The Olympics! Every amateur athlete's dream. The Olympics are an international sports competition, held every four years in a different country. Only the best athletes from a country are allowed to enter the games, and the winner in each sporting event is awarded a Gold Medal. The medal signifies that the individual athlete who won it is not only the best in that sport, but that the country he is representing is also the best. So a Gold Medal is both an individual and a national honor.

The whole town of Louisville was buzzing with the news that Cassius was going to the Olympics in the summer of 1960.

"Odessa," said a neighbor to Mrs. Clay, "is it true that our Cash is going to Rome to play in the Olympics?"

"That's right," Mrs. Clay said proudly. "I'm getting things ready for the trip now. He'll be leaving sometime around the first of July."

Cassius had graduated from high school in June of 1960, with a D grade average. He ranked 367 out of 391 in his class, and really was only allowed to graduate because he had been selected to be on the American boxing team in the Olympics. It wouldn't look good for an American athlete in the Olympics to have flunked high school!

Since many athletes who enter the Olympics go on to become professional athletes, there was no doubt that Cassius, with his exceptional boxing abilities, would go professional after the Olympics. He was swamped with offers from people who wanted to manage his boxing career.

One offer that Cassius considered seriously was from R. J. Reynolds, the richest man in Louisville. The Reynolds family had made its fortune in aluminum products, and R. J. Reynolds saw that more money could be made in managing a young Black boxer.

Cassius spent the summer months just before the Olympics working around Reynolds's huge, luxurious estate. He mopped floors, dumped garbage, cleaned toilets, and swept the porch. He also ate his meals on the back porch with the family's dogs!

Cassius seldom saw Reynolds during the summer he worked for him. And although people kept telling Cassius how lucky he was to have a millionaire for a manager, he began to wonder what kind of manager would let him eat with dogs.

Those summer days in 1960 seemed to creep by. But finally the time for leaving arrived. Cassius was horrified when he learned he would be *flying* to Rome. He had never been on a plane, and it was the one thing that truly scared him.

"Do I have to fly?" he wailed to Martin, who would be accompanying him to Italy.

"Well, I tell you," Martin replied. "You can fly and get there with everybody else, or you can take a boat, which will get you to Rome in about two weeks. By then the games will be over, and you will have arrived just in time to turn around and come right back." He paused, giving Cassius a chance to let that sink in. "Now what's it gonna be?" he finally asked.

"Okay, okay," Cassius said through clenched teeth. "I'll fly if I gotta!"

Once he arrived in Rome, however, Cassius forgot all about his fear of flying. The Olympic Village, where all the athletes were staying, was filled with young people from all over the world. Like Cassius, each one was considered one of the best athletes in the country he was representing. Cassius ran around the village talking to everybody, even those whose language he couldn't speak. That didn't matter. For a natural talker such as Cassius, there is always a way to make yourself understood.

As usual, he began bragging. He received a five-dollar money order from back home and claimed it was a five-thousand-dollar check from his millionaire manager. "Look!" he yelled, waving the money order toward anyone who would look. "My manager done sent me five thousand dollars!"

On the opening day of the Olympics, Cassius marched with the rest of the American team around the Roman Coliseum. Dressed in starched white pants and a navy blue blazer with a tiny American flag on the lapel, Cassius marched proudly and silently before the thousands of the people in the stands, who were cheering as each country's team delegation passed by.

Nineteen countries had entered the light heavyweight division of the boxing games — the division in which Cassius was fighting. Many of the boxers Cassius fought were older, more experienced men. But Cassius beat all of them to qualify for the finals.

In the finals Cassius would be fighting a Polish boxer named Zbigniew Pietrzykowski who had fought over 230 fights. He was also left-handed, the one trait in a boxer that gave Cassius some trouble. Two of his amateur fight losses had been to left-handers.

The bell sounded for round one. Cassius was already having difficulty with Pietrzykowski's style. But by the middle of round two Cassius was getting used to the Pole's style and started to take command. He smashed him two times quickly in the face, making him bleed. During

Cassius arrives home from the Olympics a hero, welcomed by his brother, Rudolph, and mother and father, Odessa and Cassius Clay, Sr. (UPI PHOTO)

the last round, Cassius's opponent was sagging against the ropes with blood dripping from his nose, mouth, and around his eyes. Cassius was clearly the winner.

When the bell sounded ending the fight, a cheer went up from the stands. The announcer got on the loudspeaker and said: "Ladies and gentlemen, the winner in the light heavyweight boxing competition is Cassius Clay, representing the United States of America!" Another cheer went up in the stands. Cassius had just won the Gold

Displaying his new Gold Medal, Cassius is surrounded by students from his high school, Central High.
(COURIER JOURNAL AND LOUISVILLE TIMES)

Medal for himself and for his country — the highest honor in amateur sports competition!

As Cassius stood on a platform between the second- and third-place winners, an Olympic official hung the shiny Gold Medal around his neck. For once he was speechless.

But later that evening and throughout the rest of the Olympics, Cassius showed off his medal everywhere. To all of Rome, he announced, "I told you, I told you, didn't I? I *am* the greatest!"

Cassius received a hero's welcome when he returned home. His mother and father and brother Rudy were at the airport to meet him, along with a police escort that led him through a parade downtown. Black and white crowds lined the streets, and when the parade passed Central High, there was a giant sign stretched across the front which read: "Welcome home, Cassius."

The mayor of Louisville gave him the key to the city. The governor of Kentucky shook his hand and told him he should be proud of the name Cassius Clay. The steps of Cassius's porch at home had been painted red, white, and blue, and American flags were flying in the yard. Cassius and his father stood on the porch arm in arm, while Mr. Clay sang "The Star-Spangled Banner," and the photographers snapped away with their cameras. Cassius was truly proud of that moment. Proud of having won the Gold Medal. Proud of representing his country. And proud of being an American.

Right after winning the medal in Rome, a Russian reporter asked Cassius how it felt to represent a country where Black people often were not allowed to eat at the same table with white people.

Cassius became furious. "I ain't worried," he snapped. "We got qualified people working on that. And anyhow, I ain't eating alligators or living in a mud hut."

Cassius would soon regret that comment. But standing on the porch, arm in arm with his father, he didn't realize how soon.

Offers from people who wanted to be Cassius's manager

came pouring in after he returned from Rome. Former heavyweight champions Archie Moore and Rocky Marciano both wanted to manage him. Cassius wanted either Joe Louis or Sugar Ray Robinson, but neither was interested.

He finally accepted the offer of ten Louisville millionaire businessmen, who proposed managing him together. Under the terms, Cassius received a $10,000 bonus for signing the six-year contract. He would get $200 a month for the first two years, then $6,000 a year for the next four years. In addition, he would receive half of any earnings from his fights. His managers, who called themselves the "Louisville Sponsoring Group," would pay trainers' salaries and other expenses. In addition, 15 percent of Cassius's earnings would go into a pension fund that he could not touch until he was thirty-five years old.

It wasn't a bad deal for an eighteen-year-old kid. Cassius took part of his $10,000 bonus and bought himself a pink Cadillac. The rest he gave to his parents to be used for house repairs.

The Gold Medal that Cassius won at the Olympics was his most prized possession. He kept it with him all the time: when he ate, when he slept, even when he bathed. After a while the "gold" started to peel, showing that it wasn't real gold at all, but gold plate. It didn't matter. To Cassius it was his symbol of greatness — but that was before some members of a motorcycle gang tried to take it away from him.

Shortly after Cassius returned from Rome, he and his

buddy Ronnie King were riding their motorbikes through downtown Louisville. The sky turned cloudy, looking as though it would rain any minute. Cassius slowed down in front of a restaurant, next to a row of parked Harley-Davidson motorcycles. They were huge, sleek machines, done up in chrome and leather. The bike owners were seated near a window in the restaurant looking at Cassius. All of them were white, dressed in leather jackets with Nazi emblems and the Confederate flag stitched across the backs.

"C'mon," Cassius said to Ronnie. "Let's go in. It's startin' to rain, and I'm hungry."

"Not in there!" Ronnie cried, sounding worried. Like many cities in the South in the early sixties, Louisville was a segregated city that did not allow Blacks in many of its public places.

"What are you talking about?" Cassius said, sounding impatient. "I'm hungry!"

Ronnie followed Cassius into the restaurant, and the two of them took seats not too far from the motorcycle gang. Cassius recognized one of the gang members. He was known as Kentucky Slim. The leader of the gang was named Frog. He was a big redhead who had his plump blond girlfriend leaning on one shoulder, and heavy leg chains hanging from the other one.

Cassius and Ronnie decided to order hamburgers and milkshakes. But when the waitress came over to the table, she told them as nicely and as quietly as possible that the restaurant did not serve Black people.

"What!" Ronnie shouted, not wanting his fear to show. "Don't you know who this is?" he said, pointing to Cassius. "This is Cassius Clay, who just won the Gold Medal in Rome. Show 'em your medal, Cash."

"Shut up, Ronnie," Cassius said quietly. He was feeling embarrassed. Why should he have to show a Gold Medal in order to get a hamburger and milkshake?

Suddenly the owner of the restaurant came out from behind the counter. "I don't care who the hell he is!" he bellowed at Ronnie. "We don't serve niggers in here!"

Ronnie couldn't believe it. "Call your millionaire managers," he urged Cassius. "Tell them what's happening. They'll close this place down!"

Cassius went to the phone booth to make the call. He stopped. *What exactly do I want these white men to do?* he thought. *Make the owner give me a hamburger?* Cassius couldn't make the call. *I didn't need their permission to win the Gold Medal, so I sure ain't gonna ask for it to get something to eat.*

"Come on," he yelled to Ronnie when he came out of the booth. "Let's go."

"But Cash . . ."

"Come *on,* I said."

Cassius's stomach was turning. He was humiliated. He had just won the Gold Medal for his country, and was now being told he couldn't sit down in a restaurant in his country to eat a fifty-cent hamburger.

"Hey, Olympic nigger," came a voice behind Cassius. "You still trying to get a milkshake?"

Cassius turned and saw Kentucky Slim and Frog with his girlfriend. They and the rest of the gang were climbing on their bikes. They gunned the motors . . . Varooooom! R-r-ro-o-o-om! and roared past Ronnie and Cassius, who were on their bikes.

Suddenly, Kentucky Slim broke away from the gang and drove back toward Cassius. "Listen," he said with a wheezing sound. "Frog wanted to lynch ya'all back in there, but I wouldn't let him. I told him, 'No suh, let that nigger boy alone, just get him to give you his medal as a souvenir, that's all.'"

Cassius's hand clutched his medal instinctively.

"You tell Frog we'll give him the medal for his mama," Ronnie yelled, gunning his bike.

"You gonna be sorry you said that, nigger boy! You hear me! You gonna be sorry!" Kentucky Slim shouted, heading back to the gang.

Cassius and Ronnie stepped on the gas and roared down the road. They knew the gang was following, and Ronnie told Cassius to go ahead since he was the one the gang wanted. Ronnie's plan was to try to head them off before they got to Cassius.

They were nearing the Ohio River. Cassius moved out ahead of Ronnie. When Frog's bike drew up next to Ronnie's, Ronnie leaped off his bike onto Frog's, knocking them both on the ground, along with Frog's girlfriend, who was riding behind him on the bike.

Ronnie pulled a knife and put it to Frog's throat. "Tell your men to back off!" he snarled.

Kentucky Slim, meanwhile, had caught up with Cassius and tried to knock him off the bike with his doubled-up leg chains. He missed, and Cassius knocked his hand, causing them both to fall over, hitting their heads together. Then Cassius put his fist in Kentucky Slim's face.

Ronnie still had his knife at Frog's throat when Cassius circled back to find him. "Tell your gang to get outa here!" he was screaming at Frog.

"We're going, we're going!" cried Frog's girlfriend. "Just don't kill Frog. Please! We're going and we won't come back!"

Ronnie let Frog go, and he and his girlfriend jumped on his bent-up bike and took off.

Cassius and Ronnie stood for a minute looking at each other after the gang had left. "We'd better go down to the river and wash off," Ronnie said, staring at Cassius. "Hey," he suddenly blurted. "You hurt?"

Cassius shook his head. He wasn't hurt physically. But the sickness he had felt in his stomach earlier had returned. He took off his Gold Medal before washing himself, and hung it on a piece of wood. Then he took a long, hard look at it. It was the first time he had taken it off since winning it. Suddenly it lost its magic for Cassius. It was just an ordinary object. He knew what he was going to do with it and already began to feel better.

After washing, Ronnie took the medal and placed it around Cassius's neck. Cassius sometimes thought Ronnie loved the medal more than he did. But before Ronnie could stop him, Cassius snatched the medal from his neck and flung it into the river.

"Oh, my God!" Ronnie wailed, horrified. "You know what you did?"

"It wasn't real gold," Cassius said, trying to put his arms around Ronnie. "It was phony."

But Ronnie wouldn't listen, and moved away from Cassius's touch. "You threw your medal in the river! Why? Why?" he kept asking.

Cassius couldn't really explain it himself. The medal had once been his most prized possession. It was the one thing that proved to his former teachers and his school friends that he was a winner, even if he wasn't academically smart. It proved that he belonged to a team, a country, a world.

But it wasn't enough. He had returned home from Rome a hero, an all-American boy who had made good internationally. Only to find that he couldn't even get a hamburger and a milkshake in a diner! Something was wrong. Now, standing on the bridge overlooking the river, Cassius watched his medal sink into the muddy water, and suddenly felt relief. He would be a champion all right, he thought to himself. "But I'll be my own kind of champion."

4
In This Corner, Allah!

There was once a man named Cassius Clay,
He fought for the title and came a long way.
He became a Muslim, changed his name,
As Muhammad Ali, he grew proud of his fame.
— *Shelly Sykes,*
nine years old

It was February 26, 1964, the day after Cassius Clay astonished the world with his knockout victory over Sonny Liston. Cassius had called a press conference, and the room was jammed with reporters, microphones, and television cameras.

He had an announcement to make — very brief and to the point: "Everything with common sense wants to be with its own," he began. "Bluebirds want to be with bluebirds. Pigeons want to be with pigeons. Tigers want to be with tigers."

Then he delivered the blow: "I believe in the religion of Islam. I believe there is no God but Allah. This is the same religion that is believed by over seven hundred million dark-skinned people throughout Africa and Asia." Cassius also announced he was dropping his last name and would now be known as Cassius X.

A stunned hush fell over the room. Cassius's statement

had the effect of a knockout punch. He was publicly announcing to the people gathered before him, to the country, and to the world, that he was a Black Muslim.

At the time, Black Muslims in America were considered racist. They were thought to be militant and violent, and bent on destroying whites. They preached separation of the black and white races. They didn't believe in working within, or even in being a part of the system.

Now, Cassius Clay was stating that he was a member of this group! The American public was thunderstruck. It was one thing to be a big-mouthed, flashy athlete who brought excitement to the sport of boxing. It was quite another thing to be a serious, dedicated member of an organization that was telling America where it could go. Especially if that serious and dedicated member also happened to be the newly crowned world heavyweight champion. The world heavyweight champion a Black Muslim? Not if the boxing world had anything to say about it.

Three days before his scheduled fight with Sonny Liston, Cassius's trainer, Angelo Dundee, burst into Cassius's dressing room in Miami's Fifth Street Gym, with a look of horror on his face.

"Do you know who's out there?" he asked Cassius, pointing toward the gym. "Malcolm X!"

Malcolm X was the leading spokesman for the Nation of Islam, as the Black Muslims in America are called. He was a fiery, eloquent speaker who had attracted attention and notoriety with his verbal attacks on America.

"I know he's out there," Cassius responded calmly to Dundee's question. "I invited him. He's a friend of mine."

"So it's true," Dundee said with a sigh. There had been rumors that Cassius was associating with Black Muslims. One of his closest friends was a man called Captain Samuels, a Black Muslim minister. And the women hired to cook for Cassius at his training camp were also members of the Nation of Islam.

"Do you know what the newspapers will do if they find out you're associated with the Muslims?" Dundee said, almost shouting. "They'll tear you apart. Your career will be finished! We've got to get Malcolm X out of here!"

But Cassius paid no attention to Dundee, and the trainer quickly left the room.

A few hours later Cassius received a call from Bill McDonald, the promoter of the Clay-Liston fight. He had just heard about Cassius's connection with the Black Muslims, and demanded to see him in his office immediately.

"If you don't make a public statement denying your association with the Black Muslims, the fight is off," McDonald told Cassius when he arrived at his office.

Cassius sensed that McDonald wasn't kidding, but, then, neither was he. He stood up and looked intently at McDonald. "I can't denounce my religion," he said quietly. "I know I can beat Liston, and I don't want to call the fight off, but if you have to call it off because of my faith, then the fight's off."

McDonald became angry. His phone rang, and when he picked it up he told the caller on the other end that the fight was being canceled. "Tell the press," he said. "Tell everybody the fight is off."

Cassius turned and walked out of the office, followed by Chris Dundee, Angelo's brother, who pleaded with Cassius to make a statement rejecting the Black Muslim religion.

When Cassius arrived home, he received a call from one of his Louisville sponsors, who also pleaded with him to make the statement. "What've you got to lose?" the sponsor argued. "And they'll never give you a chance like this again!"

Cassius knew his sponsor was right about this being his last chance to fight Liston. And deep down he was shaken up, because he knew McDonald really would cancel the fight. Still, there was more at stake than a title shot and the heavyweight championship.

"I'm not going to denounce my religion," Cassius told the sponsor. "Not even for the fight."

The sponsor became frantic, telling Cassius that he could still believe in Allah — privately — if he would just denounce Him publicly. "Allah will understand," the sponsor said. Then he abruptly hung up.

Cassius suddenly felt very alone. No one understood that his membership in the Nation of Islam was a very serious commitment, not to be taken lightly or discarded because it might jeopardize his career. For Cassius, the Islam religion had become more than something you practiced once a week. It was a way of life. He couldn't denounce it. He wouldn't.

Most of Cassius's staff members had learned of Clay's

conversation with the sponsor, and waited expectantly for a word from Cassius.

"What are we gonna do now?" his friend Bundini finally asked.

"We're going home to Louisville," Cassius said wearily. "The fight's off, and that means you get no money."

"It means you ain't no phony!" Bundini shouted back. "I stay with you, money or no money!"

Cassius and his staff packed up their equipment and loaded it into the bus, Big Red, which would take them back to Louisville. Just as Cassius was about to start the bus, he told Bundini to make one last check of the house to be sure they got everything. Bundini went in, and quickly came running back out.

"There's a phone call!" he yelled to Cassius.

The call was from Chris Dundee. "The fight's back on!" he said happily to Cassius. "Everybody talked to McDonald and he's gonna have it. You don't have to disavow your religion!"

"That's the only way I'd do it," Cassius replied.

Cassius had refused to back down, and he won. In some ways it was a greater victory than the one he was to score over Sonny Liston three days later.

Cassius's managers and trainers and sponsors believed his interest in the Islam religion had come about recently, arising in the last few months before his fight with Liston. Actually, Cassius had become interested in the religion shortly after he won the Gold Medal in 1960. His brother,

Rudy, had joined the Nation, and for some time he kept telling Cassius how much it had changed his life.

One day in the early sixties Cassius was training for a fight in Miami, when a polite and neatly dressed Black man who said he was a Muslim minister stopped by the gym to talk to Cassius.

"Would you like to come to my mosque and hear about the history of our African forefathers?" the minister asked. Cassius was surprised. The only forefathers he heard of Black people having were slaves. So, out of curiosity, he agreed to come to the meeting.

Later that evening in the mosque (an Islamic temple) Cassius sat fascinated, listening to the Black Muslim minister.

"There is no such thing as *Negro* people!" the minister said emphatically, waving his hand with a flourish. He was a strong, forceful speaker with a voice that seemed to hypnotize the audience.

"Chinese people are named after China," he continued. "Cubans are named after Cuba, Jamaicans are named after Jamaica. Now, what country does the term 'Negroes' come from?" he asked. "Why are *we* called Negroes?"

Cassius was amazed. "Why *are* we called Negroes?" he wondered to himself. And then the minister said that Black people in America don't even know their names.

"If I say Mr. Chang-Chung," the minister said, "you know he's Chinese. If I say here comes Mr. Lumumba, you know he's African. But if I say here comes Mr. Cole or Mr. Smith or Mr. Washington, you don't know what color he is until you see him. You don't know if he's Black or white because all Black people in America are named after white people!"

Man, this is something! Cassius thought, listening to the minister. What was being said made so much *sense*.

"If you don't know your own name, you don't know your language, and you don't know your religion and you don't know your God!" the minister went on. By now Cassius was totally captivated.

He attended more mosque meetings, and at the end of each one came away having learned something new. He first learned that the Islam religion was practiced in the Middle East and Africa, where the majority of dark-skinned people lived. Because of this, Black Muslims in America believed Islam was a Black religion — one they could identify with as a people.

Soon, Cassius had attended enough mosque meetings to be convinced that the Black Muslim religion was the one for him, too. It gave him his first real sense of pride in belonging to a group that celebrated Blackness instead of putting it down. Cassius had felt he *belonged* as a member of an American team when he won the Gold Medal, but after all, he had found that his Blackness could still keep him from such simple dignities as getting a hamburger at a diner. Was that what *belonging* meant for Blacks in America?

Cassius also admitted that he once took great pride in his light brown skin and white man's name. But through the teachings of the Nation of Islam, he learned to glorify his

Muhammad addresses a Black Muslim annual convention, while Elijah Muhammad, the leader of the Nation of Islam, listens intently. (UPI PHOTO)

Blackness and appreciate the richness of his African past.

The Black Muslims also taught great self-discipline. Members were not allowed to drink, gamble, smoke, eat pork (which was considered poisonous to the body), or to have sex outside of marriage. As a boxer, Cassius needed enormous training and discipline to stay in top physical condition, so the Muslims' laws helped him stay in excellent shape for boxing.

The American public considered the Black Muslims racist because they opposed integration and the concept of "making it" within the established American system. Muslims even changed their American names to Arabic and African ones to signify a new identity that better reflected their heritage.

The Black Muslims believed that the only way the Black man in America could obtain real freedom was by becoming economically and socially self-sufficient the way other ethnic groups in America had done. So, under the guidance of the Honorable Elijah Muhammad, the leader of the organization, the Nation of Islam started businesses in Black communities which provided good services at reasonable prices to the people.

But in 1964, when Cassius won the world heavyweight championship and announced he was a Muslim, the majority of the American people didn't know, or care to find out, about the positive effects the Black Muslims were having on the Black community. They only knew that a Black Muslim certainly should not have been wearing the heavyweight championship crown. They'd rather have Sonny Liston as champion!

When he had first announced that he was a Black Muslim, Cassius had declared his name changed to Cassius X. (The "X" meant "unknown," since Blacks in America don't know their original African names.) About a month later, Cassius announced he was changing his name again, this time to Muhammad Ali — an Islamic name, meaning "he who is named after the prophet."

Most people were outraged. To have to call the world heavyweight champion Muhammad Ali was to show more respect for the Black Muslims than most Americans could stomach. The general reaction to the fighter's Black Muslim membership was quick and hostile. Former heavyweight champion Joe Louis said: "Clay will earn the public's hatred because of his connection with the Black Muslims. The things they preach are just the opposite of what we believe."

Dr. Martin Luther King, Jr., the respected civil rights leader who advocated integration, said: "Cassius [has become] a champion of racial segregation. I think [he] should spend more time proving his boxing skill and do less talking."

One of the Louisville sponsors said, simply, that the champ had been "brainwashed."

"Of all the reactions, the one that most irritated Cassius or "Muhammad," as he will be called from now on, was the one that came from Floyd Patterson, who had lost his crown to Sonny Liston. "I'm proud to be an American," Patterson said, "and proud of my people, and no one group of people could make me change my views." He then challenged Muhammad to a fight as if he wanted to prove his point in the ring — "for all people who think and feel as I do," he said.

The president of the World Boxing Association wanted to strip Muhammad of his boxing title because of his Black Muslim membership. "Clay is a detriment to the boxing world," he said. "His general conduct is provoking worldwide criticism and is setting a very poor example for the youth of the world."

Muhammad was enraged when he heard this. Nobody had threatened to strip Sonny Liston of his title when he was champion, and he had been a convict. Muhammad fought clean, honest fights, didn't drink or smoke or gamble, and had never been in trouble with the law. He was certainly a much better example for youth than Liston had been.

Muhammad agreed to a rematch fight with Liston to prove his win had not been an accident. He was certain he could whip Liston a second time.

In June of 1964, Muhammad married a lovely model named Sonji Roi, and the two of them went on a tour of Africa. The response to Muhammad Ali in Africa was just the opposite of what it had been in America. Since many of the countries that Muhammad visited in Africa followed the Islam religion, there he received a hero's welcome and royal treatment. He was the first Muslim to win a world

Cassius, after knocking Liston to the floor during their second fight in 1965, dares him to get up. (UPI PHOTO)

championship, and the Africans loved him for it. They also loved him for refusing to give in to the pressure back in the States to reject his religion.

When Muhammad returned to America, he started training for his second match with Liston. And on May 25, 1965, in Lewiston, Maine, Muhammad Ali faced Sonny Liston for the second time.

The fight was over in the first three minutes of the first

round. Ali threw a punch that was so quick Liston didn't even see it — he only felt it as he hit the mat. It all happened so fast that the audience thought the fight had been fixed. But Muhammad had simply shown, for the second time, that he was the superior fighter. He was now unquestionably and undisputedly the world heavyweight champion.

Now Muhammad was ready to take on Floyd Patterson, who had earlier challenged him to a fight. Even though he was Black, Patterson represented America's "Great White Hope" in his match with Ali; he had vowed to return the heavyweight crown to Christianity, and would be fighting for all the values America symbolized. Interestingly, Patterson was the first of several Black "white hopes" who would fight Ali during his controversial career.

To Muhammad, Patterson and others like him represented the worst kind of Blacks — those who would allow themselves to be used by whites against other Blacks. Muhammad called Patterson a "rabbit," and never failed to mention that Patterson had been forced to move out of an all-white neighborhood in New York because he was Black!

"I'm not forcing myself into places where I'm not wanted," Ali said. "I'm staying with my own, and I want to be with my own, and do all I can for my own."

When Ali finally faced Patterson in Las Vegas for their fight on November 22, 1965, he spent eleven rounds bullying and playing with the former champion just to show how little he thought of him. During the twelfth round,

Ali finished Patterson off. It was a humiliating defeat for Patterson.

With the second Liston defeat and the Patterson loss combined, the public was forced to recognize Ali as champion, which also meant, like it or not, acknowledging him as a Black Muslim.

For Muhammad Ali it was a double victory. He had not only regained the crown, but had withstood the public's challenge to his Islam faith. He had gone round one with the American Establishment and won. It seemed Allah was in his corner. But round two was coming up, and this time the challenger in the opposite corner would be Uncle Sam's army.

5
"No Viet Cong Ever Called Me Nigger"

Keep asking me, no matter how long
On the war in Viet Nam, I sing this song
I ain't got no quarrel with the Viet Cong.
— *Muhammad Ali*

The army induction center near Miami was hot that day in January 1964. Muhammad, along with several other young men sitting in the room, was sweating as he waited nervously for his number to be called. The men had all been ordered to report to the center for their physicals and intelligence tests, which would determine whether or not they were eligible for military service.

"Number 15-47-42-127!" an officer called out. "Come forward!"

Muhammad got up from his seat and approached the desk where the officer was sitting.

"What's this?" the officer asked suspiciously, as he showed Muhammad his army forms. Muhammad had signed the forms "Cassius X." Although he had not yet made his public statement announcing his membership in the Nation of Islam, Muhammad had already joined the group by the time he was ordered to report to the induction center. (It would be another couple of months before he would declare himself Muhammad Ali.)

"I practice the Islamic religion," Muhammad politely told the army officer. Then he explained why he used the "X."

The officer was still suspicious and ordered Muhammad to come into another room. There he showed him a list of political organizations considered dangerous by the United States government. "Do you belong to any of these groups?" the officer asked.

"No, sir," Muhammad replied, looking at the list. The Nation of Islam was not on it.

"All right," the officer said, apparently satisfied. He sent Muhammad to another room for his physical exam. Since Muhammad was in superior condition (he was in training for his forthcoming fight with Liston), he passed his physical test easily.

In the next room, however, Muhammad faced a much more difficult test — the army's qualifying test, which measured intelligence. This room had desks and chairs, and on top of each desk was a pencil and booklet containing questions. The answers to the questions were to be marked on a separate piece of paper.

Muhammad sat staring at the questions. He had always been a poor reader, and besides, from what he could read he realized he had no idea of what any of the answers were. He guessed at most of them.

The tests were graded right after each man finished.

Muhammad scored 16. He had to score 30 in order to pass.

"You've flunked the intelligence test," an officer bluntly told Muhammad after grading his test. His draft status would now be changed from 1-A to 1-Y, which meant he would not have to serve in the military. The army had decided he wasn't smart enough for them!

It was just as well, Muhammad thought, since he had no intention of serving in the army, even if he had passed the test. As a member of the Nation of Islam, he had planned to declare himself a conscientious objector on religious grounds. Conscientious objectors do not have to serve in the military if they can prove that military service would conflict with their moral or religious principles.

Since the Black Muslims opposed participation by any of their members in American organizations, Muhammad would certainly not participate in what the Nation of Islam considered the worst American organization of all — the military.

Also, in 1964 the war in Viet Nam was escalating, with America sending more and more young men overseas to fight. As far as the Black Muslims were concerned, America was fighting a racist war in Viet Nam. The Vietnamese were yellow-skinned Asians. No Black Muslim was going to fight another man of color for the American government!

Fortunately, Muhammad did not have to claim conscientious objector status in 1964 because of his 1-Y draft classification. But a few months after taking the intelligence test in Miami, he was ordered to take another one, this time in Louisville, Kentucky. (Since Muhammad had been born in Louisville, the draft board there could make him take the test again.)

Muhammad reported to the Louisville draft board as ordered, and took the test again. He flunked it again, and his draft status remained 1-Y.

Public reaction to Muhammad continued to be hostile after he defeated Liston and changed his name. People still didn't like the idea of a Black Muslim being heavyweight champion, especially one who was as brash and arrogant as Muhammad. The World Boxing Association had taken away Muhammad's title in 1965, charging that his second fight with Liston was illegal due to a contract technicality. The WBA declared that the real champion was a man named Ernie Terrell, a tall Black boxer from Texas who hadn't even fought Muhammad! Not much attention was paid to the WBA's pronouncements, however.

After Muhammad flunked the army test a second time and was declared exempt from military service, letters began to pour into the Louisville draft board from angry Americans around the country.

"How much has Clay paid you to keep him out of the army?" one letter asked.

"That nigger is no better than everybody else. Draft his butt," another letter ordered.

"When are you going to have the guts to bring that lousy, loudmouthed, un-American, cowardly nigger back home and put him in the army where we all hope he'll have his head shot off?" wrote another, who went on to denounce the idea of Muhammad earning money on his fights in Europe instead of fighting in Viet Nam!

Muhammad was not only a Black Muslim and a loudmouth; he was becoming rich. By 1966, at twenty-four years of age, he had made over two million dollars! The public couldn't stand it. Who did he think he was? Muhammad always had just one answer to that question: "I'm the greatest!"

But the Greatest was also becoming a threat, not just to the American public, but also to those whites who had traditionally controlled the sport of boxing — many of whom were involved in organized crime. It was common knowledge in boxing that heavyweight champions were frequently under the influence of crime figures who made a lot of money from championship fights.

This wasn't the case with Muhammad. When his contract with the Louisville sponsoring group expired in the fall of 1966, Herbert Muhammad, the son of the Black Muslims' leader Elijah Muhammad, became Muhammad's new manager. Even before his Louisville contract was up, Muhammad Ali began organizing a group of boxing promoters, which, for the first time in the history of boxing, included Blacks. He was determined that more Blacks — not just boxers — should have an opportunity to make money in professional boxing, especially since most of the champion boxers were Black!

Muhammad was becoming just what he said he would be: "My own kind of champion." That was the promise he had made to himself years ago when he threw his Gold Medal into the Ohio River. "I don't have to be what you want me to be," he would defiantly tell the whites who were used to having Black fighters jump to their commands.

So, with Muhammad Ali wearing the heavyweight crown, some of the control of boxing was beginning to pass from white hands into Black ones. To boxing officials, promoters, and sportswriters, that was worse than mob control!

However, it looked as though Muhammad, like Sonny Liston, was going to be champion for as long as he wanted, and that meant he would continue to play the game by his rules. Unless, of course, Muhammad's enemies could find a way to interrupt the game. They succeeded. A letter from the President of the United States, addressed to "Cassius Clay, also known as Muhammad Ali," was delivered to Muhammad on April Fool's Day in 1967. He was living in Houston, Texas, where he had been training for a fight with Ernie Terrell, the declared WBA champion.

The letter contained an order from President Lyndon B. Johnson that Muhammad report to the Houston draft board on April 28, 1967 at 8:30 A.M. to be drafted into the armed services!

Muhammad's draft status had been changed from 1-Y to 1-A in 1966, two years after he flunked the army qualifying test a second time. News of this had come to Muhammad while he was living in Miami, from a television reporter who had brought along his camera crew.

"Hey, Champ!" the reporter had called to Muhammad, who was relaxing in a lounge chair in the yard of his rented home. "Champ, you've been reclassified 1-A by the draft board," the reporter told Muhammad.

The film crew had the cameras set up and zoomed in for a close-up of Muhammad's reaction.

"What?" Muhammad said, sitting up. "What'd you say?"

"I said you've been reclassified 1-A. The army lowered the passing score on its qualifying test from 30 to 15. That now makes you eligible for service."

Muhammad was stunned. "How can they do this?" he asked. "Why are they gunning for me? I ain't got no quarrel with them Viet Congs!"

I ain't got no quarrels with them Viet Congs! That statement flashed on every newscast and appeared in every newspaper in the country that evening, and it sent shock waves through America. The war in Viet Nam was growing in size and also in unpopularity.

On the one hand, there were thousands of Americans who believed it was all right for the country to be fighting in Viet Nam, simply because the military said it was all right. Even though many of these same Americans had lost husbands or sons in the war, they had not stopped to question why their husbands or sons were in Viet Nam in the first place. They gasped when they heard Muhammad's statement.

On the other hand, there was an increasing number of people, most of them young, who had begun to question the war. They believed the South Vietnamese and the

North Vietnamese (the Viet Cong) were essentially engaged in a civil war, one in which America had no business fighting. The government claimed it had made a commitment to fight on the side of the South Vietnamese. But many young Americans felt the United States army should get out of Viet Nam altogether. They cheered when they heard Muhammad's comment. They didn't have any quarrel with the Viet Cong, either.

But in 1966 the young people in the antiwar movement were still a minority. Most Americans didn't *want* to start questioning the war, since it meant they might have to admit that their sons and husbands were fighting and possibly dying for nothing.

A few days after making his statement, Muhammad made another one: "No Viet Cong ever called me nigger," he said simply. Why should he go halfway around the world to fight in a senseless war? He knew his real enemies were those in America who robbed Blacks of their pride and civil rights.

Muhammad's statements turned into political dynamite. He was called a traitor and a "tool of Hanoi" (Hanoi being the capital of North Viet Nam). Several of his boxing matches were transferred to Europe and Canada because boxing commissioners in this country would not allow him to fight in their states. The Louisville draft board was bombarded with more letters from enraged Americans demanding that Muhammad be drafted.

Muhammad applied for conscientious objector status with the Louisville draft board after he was notified of his

1-A reclassification. He was turned down. The board refused to recognize the Nation of Islam as a legitimate religion, which meant that Muhammad could not plead conscientious objection on religious grounds.

The battle lines were being drawn. Muhammad's lawyers appealed the draft board's decision. They lost but continued to appeal.

Privately, Muhammad was promised that if he served in the army, he would not be sent to Viet Nam. He could spend his two years of duty competing in army boxing exhibitions, he was told, just like Joe Louis did. "No," Muhammad said. "I'm not going."

Then on April 1, 1967, Muhammad received his orders from the President of the United States: report to the Houston induction center on April 28 to be drafted into the army.

Muhammad's lawyers immediately appealed to the Houston draft board for his exemption as a conscientious objector, but they were turned down. One of Muhammad's lawyers called to tell him the news. "It looks like trouble, Champ," he said. "You're not going to be deferred. This isn't like any case I've ever had. Joe Namath can get out of going into the army to play football, but with you it's different. They want to make an example of you."

Muhammad understood. If he refused to step forward when his name was called at Houston's induction center on April 28, he would be breaking the law. He could be sent to jail.

If he did step forward, he would be violating his principles as a Black Muslim. Stepping forward would also indicate that he supported the U.S. army and the war it was fighting in Viet Nam.

On February 6, 1967, Muhammad defeated Ernie Terrell in Houston and finally got belated recognition from the WBA as world champion. But people were more interested in the confrontation he was to have two months later in the induction center.

"What are you going to do, Champ?" people would ask him on the street. "Are you going to take that step?"

"Don't take the step, Champ!" others would say. "Don't go! Don't go!"

Muhammad was beginning to become a political symbol to those who opposed the war in Viet Nam. A growing number of Blacks began to admire him for his courage in standing up for what he believed. As the day approached when Muhammad was due to report to the induction center, no one was certain of what the champ would do when he was ordered to step forward. Would he refuse to take the step, and risk jail? Or would he give in, and spend his two years in the army in some comfortable job? No one knew, and Muhammad wasn't saying.

On the night of April 27, the evening before Muhammad was scheduled to appear at the induction center, sportscaster Howard Cosell arrived at Muhammad's hotel in Houston for an interview. Muhammad and Cosell had become friends over the years. Although they teased and taunted each other publicly on television, each also came to have a deep respect for the other. Cosell was the only sports commentator who immediately honored Muhammad's Black Muslim religion by calling him "Ali" when he changed his name.

Now, Cosell wanted to know from Muhammad whether he would take the step the next day.

"Can't tell you a thing, Cosell," Muhammad said when the sportscaster entered the room. Muhammad was sprawled on his hotel bed watching television.

"I understand," Cosell said. "But I have a camera crew here."

"You won't get a word out of me," Muhammad responded casually. He told Cosell he had been instructed by Elijah Muhammad, the leader of the Nation of Islam, not to say anything to the press about his decision. "I can't tell you *anything*."

Realizing he would get nowhere, Cosell finally left the room. He recalls now that Muhammad was still lying across the bed, staring at the television. He appeared totally untroubled.

The next morning the streets and sidewalks were jammed with people waiting outside the induction center for Muhammad to arrive. Some Black students from Texas Southern University were marching with banners that said "Stay Home, Muhammad Ali!"

At about 8:15 a taxicab pulled up in front of the building. When the crowd spotted Muhammad sitting in the back of the cab, it began to scream: "Muhammad Ali! Muhammad Ali! *Don't go!*"

Standing across the street was H. Rap Brown, the militant civil rights leader, who had a clenched fist raised and was shouting, along with other Blacks, "Hep! Hep! Don't take that step! Hep! Hep! Don't take that step!" Another group of men — young whites, many with beards and long hair — were also shouting, "We didn't go! You don't go! We didn't go! You don't go!"

Muhammad got out of the cab and the crowd pushed toward him. "Stand up, brother! We're with you," cried an old woman, grabbing Muhammad's hand. "Fight for us. Don't let us down!"

Policemen began to push people away from the door to the center so Muhammad could go in. They were holding back newspaper reporters and photographers, who were yelling, "Muhammad, give us the answer! Are you going in? What will your stand be?"

Muhammad was finally able to make it to the top of the induction center steps, and just before going inside, he turned around to look at the people below. Hundreds of them — Black and white, old and young — had turned out in the early hours of the morning to offer words of support and encouragement for the action he was about to take.

Inside, Muhammad was escorted to a large room filled with about thirty other men who were being drafted. Everyone in the room was watching Muhammad. Most of the men were dressed in casual clothes, since right after the examinations they would be boarding a bus and taken to a training camp. Muhammad, however, was wearing his best black suit with a white shirt and black tie.

An officer told the men that they would first take a written test, then a physical, and finally they would be called for induction. "After that, you will line up outside for the bus to camp," he said.

Muhammad followed the other draftees through the routine of taking the written test and the physical. Then they were given a lunch break. During lunch, many of the young draftees started talking to Muhammad. Like Muhammad, they didn't want to go into the service, but they were afraid to refuse. "Are you going?" one of them whispered. "How can I keep from going?"

Suddenly, an officer walked into the room. It was time for the induction call. Muhammad's name was third. He was instructed to go to a room where he would be formally called for induction into the military.

When Muhammad entered the room, it immediately grew quiet. A young lieutenant took his place at a podium and cleared his throat. "Attention!" he snapped. There were seven other draftees besides Muhammad in the room. They were standing in two rows, four in each row. Muhammad was in the second row.

"You are about to be inducted into the armed forces of the United States, as indicated by the service announced following your name when called," the officer said briskly. "You will take one step forward as your name and service are called, and such step will constitute your induction into the armed forces indicated."

The officer called the first name. "Jason Adams — army!" A young man stepped forward. The officer called three more names. Muhammad began to sweat. The room was suddenly filled with people — all watching him.

"Cassius Clay — army!" the officer commanded.

Muhammad, standing straight, did not move.

A few of the Black draftees began to smile. But all of the other draftees were hurriedly ordered out of the room, leaving Muhammad standing alone.

The officer called out again: "Cassius Clay! Will you please step forward and be inducted into the armed forces of the United States?" Muhammad still did not move.

Another officer, a captain, came up to Muhammad and ordered him to follow him into his office.

"I don't know why you're acting this way," the captain said, after closing his office door. "If this is your final decision, you will face criminal charges and your penalty could be five years in prison and a ten-thousand-dollar fine. I am authorized to give you a second chance to reconsider your position."

"Thank you, sir, but I don't need it," Muhammad replied.

He was ordered to go back to the room, where his name was called once more. Once more, he refused to take the step forward.

Finally, the lieutenant gave Muhammad some forms to sign explaining why he was refusing to be inducted. Muhammad explained that he was a member of the Nation of Islam and had also recently become a Black Muslim minister. Then he was escorted by the captain to a room where his lawyers were waiting.

"You are free to go now," the captain said. "You will be contacted later by the United States Attorney's office."

Outside, the waiting crowds had heard the news, and a cheer went up when Muhammad came out of the center. "We're glad you didn't go!" cried a group of Black girls, running over to Muhammad. "You didn't go, so I won't go!" said a young boy standing next to H. Rap Brown.

But there are other voices in the crowd. "You headin' straight for jail!" yelled an old white woman, who was waving a tiny American flag. "You goin' straight to jail. You ain't champ no more. You ain't gonna never be champ no more!"

Before Muhammad could answer her, one of his lawyers pulled him into a waiting cab, which sped away.

By the time Muhammad got back to his hotel, he had heard on the radio that the World Boxing Association had once again stripped him of his champion title, and planned to hold an elimination tournament to determine a new champion. Also, that same day the New York Boxing Commission took away Muhammad's license, which meant he could no longer box in New York. Other states quickly took similar action.

Muhammad left Houston the next day, flying back to Chicago, the headquarters of the Nation of Islam. He was heading into an exile from boxing that would last three years, would cost him huge sums of money in court battles, and, worst of all, would erode many of his skills as a great boxer. As the plane flew out of Houston, the old white lady's words from the day before rang in Muhammad's ears: "You goin' straight to jail. You ain't never gonna be champion no more!"

6
Out, but Not Down

> Clean out my cell,
> And take my tail to jail,
> 'Cause better to be in jail fed,
> Than to be in Viet Nam, dead.
> — *Muhammad Ali*

As promised, Muhammad heard from the United States Attorney's office shortly after he refused to be inducted. He was charged with a felony in violating the Selective Service Code and tried in the Houston Federal Court. Judge Joe A. Ingraham promptly found him guilty and gave him the maximum sentence — five years in jail and a ten-thousand-dollar fine. His lawyers would appeal the decision. In the meantime, Muhammad was free on bail, but he was also out of work.

The World Boxing Association had stripped him of his title almost the instant it was announced that Muhammad had refused to be drafted. Three months later the WBA held an elimination tournament to determine the new champion, and almost every boxer in the tournament had, at one time, been defeated by Muhammad. Sonny Liston wasn't included in the tournament, and Joe Frazier, a leading contender, refused to take part.

"Let them have the elimination bouts," Muhammad angrily told a newspaper reporter. "Everybody knows me and knows I am the champion. You see, they know who the real champion is, and all the rest is sparring partners."

As it turned out, Jimmy Ellis was declared the new world heavyweight champion. He and Muhammad had known each other since their childhood days in Louisville, and more recently they had trained together as sparring partners.

Besides being stripped of his title, Muhammad had his boxing license revoked in most states in the country, which meant he could no longer earn his living by boxing. This was not only unfair, it was constitutionally illegal, since Muhammad was being denied the right to make his living before he was even tried or found guilty for refusing induction.

Muhammad's manager and promoters worked on arranging fights for him in other countries, but the State Department abruptly took away his passport. This meant he couldn't leave the country, and yet he had not yet been convicted of any crime.

His boxing career may have been brought to a sudden halt, but Muhammad's mouth was as active as ever, and while he never publicly complained about how he was being treated, he did point out the unfairness of it.

"The power structure seems to want to starve me out," he said on a television show a short time after his passport was lifted. "I mean the punishment — five years in jail, ten-thousand-dollar fine — ain't enough. They want to stop me from working, not only in this country but out of it. You read about these things in dictatorship countries, where a man don't go along with this thing or that and he's completely not allowed to work or to earn a decent living. . . . But I rely on Allah. I leave it up to Allah."

When it appeared certain that he would not be able to box anywhere, Muhammad began to earn money by lecturing, first in Muslim mosques, where he developed skills as a Black Muslim minister, and then on college campuses around the country. He was in demand everywhere, and spoke out on everything — from the war in Viet Nam to the treatment of the American Indian.

"I'm the onliest boxer in history people ask questions like a Senator," he observed.

Muhammad was fully prepared to go to jail if he lost his court appeals. The Nation of Islam's own spiritual leader, Elijah Muhammad, had spent time in jail himself for refusing to be drafted into the army during World War II. Muhammad Ali would do no less. "I'm standing up for my people, even if I have to go to jail," he said.

But as 1967 — the first year of Muhammad's exile — drew to a close, his most pressing problem was not the prospect of jail, but his rising debts. In 1966 he had divorced his first wife, Sonji, because she would not follow the Black Muslim teachings. She was demanding twelve hundred dollars a month in alimony payments.

A little more than a year after divorcing Sonji, in August of 1967, Muhammad was married again. This time it was to a beautiful seventeen-year-old girl named Belinda

Boyd, who had grown up as a member of the Black Muslim religion. Belinda worked in a Black Muslim bakery, and her parents were close friends of Muhammad's manager, Herbert Muhammad. Although Belinda and Muhammad Ali liked each other when they first met, Herbert actually *arranged* their marriage. The Nation of Islam felt Belinda would be a proper wife for Muhammad Ali. She was a devoted member of the Nation, and not likely to disregard Black Muslim rules the way high-spirited Sonji had. By the end of 1967, Belinda was pregnant with her and Muhammad's first child, and Muhammad was now faced with the additional expense of providing for a family.

Also, his court battles were beginning to demand staggering sums of money. He had a team of lawyers appealing his conviction, but they were losing. Muhammad was willing to fight the conviction all the way to the Supreme Court, if he had to, and it looked as though it would be necessary. It would also be costly.

Muhammad, however, never once lost his hope or his spirit. "I rely on Allah," he kept saying. It was clear to those who knew him that Muhammad's Islam faith was the force that sustained him. He also had the support and encouragement of the entire Nation of Islam behind him, as well as a growing number of people who were coming to admire him for bravely accepting the consequences of his actions.

"He never complained about how he was treated by the system," Howard Cosell said admiringly, "even though he had two of his constitutional rights violated — the Fifth

Amendment, which guarantees due process of law, and the Fourteenth Amendment, equal protection under the law."

Muhammad wasn't complaining, but the new 1968 year looked dismal. He and Belinda were living in Philadelphia, barely making ends meet. His savings were wiped out, the baby was expected in a few months, and court costs were rising.

One day Muhammad wrote out a check to a plumber who had made some minor repairs in his house, and the check bounced!

"I'm sorry," Muhammad said, embarrassed, when the plumber returned the check. "That's the way things are. Have no money."

Yet, as difficult as circumstances were, Muhammad still retained his integrity. For instance, he was approached by a group of filmmakers who wanted him to star in a movie they were doing on Jack Johnson, the controversial Black heavyweight champion of the nineteen-twenties. The group offered Muhammad $400,000 to be in the film.

Jack Johnson had originally been one of Muhammad's heroes. Johnson had been a flamboyant, arrogant boxer who irritated the public with his boasting and egotism. Also, like Muhammad, Johnson would go from match to match challenging the winner to fight him. Johnson once even went to Europe to challenge a fighter!

But whereas Muhammad enraged the public when he first became a Black Muslim and then defied the draft, Johnson made America angry when he started dating and then marrying white women. He had four white wives during his stormy career, one of whom he was charged with kidnapping. He fled the country rather than stay to face the charges, which were false.

Although Muhammad and Johnson were similar, it was their differences that made Muhammad turn down the movie role. "I ain't going to play in no movie opposite no white woman," he said simply, and refused the part. Nor did Muhammad intend to flee the country the way Johnson had, even though he had several opportunities. Instead, he would stick it out, taking his chances with the courts and going to jail if all of his appeals failed.

Too much was at stake to leave. His battle against the military and the courts was no longer just a personal one. Many people began to see him as a champion for them, too — fighting for people everywhere whose human rights are abused, fighting for people too weak or afraid to speak out on injustice, fighting for everyone's right to be treated with decency and respect. Muhammad was becoming a *real* champion. Even among people who did not particularly like him as a person, he was admired for what he symbolized. As Howard Cosell said, "In the age of Richard Nixon, Muhammad Ali came to stand for something."

Such notable men as Dr. Martin Luther King, Jr., the civil rights leader who once denounced Muhammad for his Islam faith, were now defending him and his right to lead his life as he chose. Senator Robert Kennedy, brother of the former United States President, John F. Kennedy, said it was a "crime" that Muhammad was being deprived of his right to make a living.

In early 1968, when it looked as though Muhammad would never fight again, he began talking about buying some farms and becoming a farmer or starting a hamburger chain to sell "champburgers." But then a curious thing happened. Fight promoters started actively trying to get him back in the ring. Secret meetings were held with boxing commissioners in different states in an attempt to have his license restored. Managers and trainers of other boxers were talked to, in the hopes of lining up possible opponents. There was talk of some exhibition matches.

Why the sudden rush by promoters to get Muhammad boxing again? Very simply, without Muhammad Ali the sport of boxing was once again nothing. Following the elimination tournament held by the WBA to determine a new champion, there was little interest in heavyweight boxing. Most people still regarded Muhammad as the legitimate champion even if he wasn't allowed to fight. It had been his flashy personality and brash mouth which usually drew people to fights in the first place. Now, without him, there was no longer any reason to go.

Fight promoters began to feel it where it hurt the most — their wallets. With Muhammad gone from the boxing scene, they were losing money. So the only sensible solution would be to bring him back.

It was almost too much to hope for, but Muhammad hoped anyway. For all of this talk about being a farmer, he knew the only thing he really wanted to do was be a boxer. He had spent nearly his entire life boxing; it was in his blood. Now there was a chance he would fight again! All praises to Allah!

Yet getting back in the ring was not going to be easy. At first, it actually looked impossible. Although Muhammad was gaining a public following, politically he was still too hot to handle. He was on the FBI's "subversives" list, his telephone was bugged, he was often followed by agents. As a result, individual boxing commissioners were afraid to go near him, let alone restore his license.

Whenever it looked as though promoters were making some headway lining up a fight for him in a state, word would leak out, ending any further discussions of a fight. Muhammad was learning not to get his hopes up too high. He had been disappointed too often.

There had been the possibility of a fight with Joe Frazier in Miami, but when Muhammad went to Florida to discuss it, he found promoters weren't willing to pay him much money. Then promoters said they had signed up Jimmy Ellis to fight him in Florida, but that fell through. Muhammad was next set to fight Floyd Patterson in Las Vegas, but at the last minute the match was called off.

From 1968 to 1970 promoters tried to get Muhammad fights in Florida, Georgia, Washington, Pennsylvania, Michigan, Arkansas, Texas, Mississippi, Ohio, and Nevada. All of the deals and near-deals collapsed. Even the Indians on a reservation in Arizona refused to let Muhammad fight there.

Matters took a turn for the worse in 1969. Muhammad went on the Howard Cosell television sports show, and

WEIGHT: 212-230 *(Estimate)*
AGE 34

6'3"

17½

15

44

13 FIST

13½

34

26

17

9½

Tale of the Tape.

admitted to his friend that he was almost broke. Cosell asked him if he would like to fight again.

"Sure," Muhammad blurted. "I could use the money."

When word of this remark reached the Nation of Islam's leader, Elijah Muhammad, Muhammad Ali was immediately given a one-year suspension from the Nation of Islam for publicly acknowledging that he needed money and wished to return to boxing. Elijah contended that if Muhammad were truly a faithful follower of Islam, he would rely on Allah for strength and would certainly not admit before the white press that he was having a hard time financially.

Also, under the Black Muslim doctrine, boxing for money was forbidden. Muhammad had always been allowed to box because, as world champion, he represented a positive image for the Nation of Islam. However, to have him announce publicly that he wanted to make money by boxing was not acceptable to Muslim leaders.

Muhammad was not only suspended from the Nation, but Black Muslim members were told to have nothing to do with him for a year as well. Even Muhammad's own brother, Rudy, now called Rahaman Ali, stayed away from him. Herbert Muhammad, Elijah's son and Muhammad Ali's manager, chose to stay with Muhammad and he, too, was suspended.

Worse yet, Elijah Muhammad refused to recognize Muhammad as Muhammad Ali. "We shall call him Cassius Clay," he said. "We take away the name of Allah from him until he proves himself worthy of that name."

It was a blow to Muhammad, but he humbly accepted the leader's decision. "I tried to mix boxing and religion," he said apologetically. "I shoulda known better." However, Muhammad would not give up his Islam name and go back to being called Cassius Clay.

In December of 1969, Muhammad tried his hand at doing professionally what he had always done naturally — acting. He starred in the Broadway musical *Buck White,* a play about a militant Black leader. While Muhammad was less than sensational in the leading role, he did get fair reviews. The *New York Times* review reported that Muhammad "emerges as a modest, naturally appealing man who sings with a pleasant slightly impersonal voice, acts without embarrassment and moves with innate dignity." The show, however, was a flop, and closed after an eight-day run.

Muhammad's suspension from the Nation of Islam was lifted in 1970, and he was welcomed back into the organization. Muhammad's lawyers also scored a victory that year. They had been working on getting his license restored in the state of New York, and when the case came before Judge Walter Mansfield in October, he ruled in Muhammad's favor. Muhammad had been denied his rights under the Fourteenth Amendment of the Constitution, which provides equal protection under the law, the judge said. In his ruling, the judge explained that the New York State Athletic Commission had been granting licenses to military *deserters,* so how could Muhammad be denied a license?

While his lawyers had been working to get his license back in New York, promoters and politicians in the state of Georgia had been waging their own campaign to arrange a fight for him. For the first time in years, it looked as though something might actually go right!

Leroy Johnson, a Black state senator from Georgia, personally appealed to the mayor of Atlanta to allow a Muhammad Ali boxing match in the city. Johnson was one of the most powerful Black politicians in Georgia, and it had been his support which enabled the mayor of Atlanta to get elected. The mayor knew it would be politically foolish to turn down a man like Johnson. He granted the request. A fight could be held in his city.

Meanwhile, Mrs. Coretta King, the widow of Dr. Martin Luther King, Jr. (who had been assassinated in 1968), Dr. Ralph Abernathy, and other respected Blacks in Georgia appealed to Governor Lester Maddox for endorsement of the fight in Georgia. Maddox, a known racist, didn't like the idea of a Muhammad Ali fight in his state, but there wasn't much he could do to stop it. The state attorney general ruled that Muhammad had to be allowed to fight.

Also, public sentiment was on the side of Muhammad. By 1970 the majority of Americans were opposed to the war in Viet Nam and had become increasingly disturbed over how Muhammad was being treated. In the city of Atlanta and other cities around the country where the majority of the population is Black, people were anxious to see Muhammad fight again. He was still recognized by them as the only legitimate world heavyweight champion.

And to Blacks, in particular, he was a different sort of champion — the "people's champion."

Governor Maddox gave in. The match would be held.

At last, Muhammad was going to fight again! But it wasn't going to be easy. Muhammad had lost more than just his heavyweight championship crown. He had lost time. To get both back, it was going to be an uphill struggle.

The newly crowned world heavyweight champion was Joe Frazier, who had defeated Jimmy Ellis in February, 1970. But before Muhammad could have a shot at a fight with Frazier, he would have to fight the leading contenders — all of whom were ahead of Muhammad in the line to Frazier.

First in line was Jerry Quarry, a big, rugged Irish American known for his ability to punch and take a punch. He and Muhammad were scheduled to face each other in Atlanta on October 26, 1970. As the date of the fight approached, all of the old excitement which Muhammad Ali had generated in the sport of boxing began to return. Promoters were billing Quarry as another Great White Hope — this time, literally white — pitted against the eternal bad boy, Muhammad Ali. A record crowd was expected to fill Atlanta Civic Auditorium.

Yet, as the day of the fight neared, tough questions were also being raised. How much had Muhammad's three-and-a-half-year exile cost him in fighting ability? Would he still have the old speed and grace? Was he still in shape? Would he make a successful comeback? Would he ever regain the heavyweight crown?

7
The Comeback

Pretenders, get off the throne!
The lamb's come to claim his own!
— *Bundini Brown*

The dirt road off the highway led to a clearing surrounded by a thick clump of fir and pine trees. A cottage, low and sprawling, sat in the clearing near the edge of a sparkling man-made lake. The cottage belonged to Leroy Johnson, the Georgia state senator who had worked so diligently to bring the Muhammad Ali–Jerry Quarry fight to his state. His efforts had paid off. The fight was scheduled to be held in Atlanta in a few weeks, at the end of October, 1970. And in a gracious tribute to the man whose comeback he had helped to ensure, Senator Johnson turned over his country cottage home to Muhammad and his crew while they were in Atlanta.

The cottage made an ideal training headquarters. It was far enough away from the city of Atlanta to be free of city distractions, yet close enough to other homes not to be totally isolated. The surrounding trees provided an atmosphere of seclusion and a feeling of privacy. It was a quiet place, a retreat where Muhammad could train and work in peace as he prepared for his comeback match.

Muhammad needed the privacy. While most sports fans and promoters and sportswriters were excitedly anticipating the Ali-Quarry fight, there were others who opposed it, especially in the South. They still saw Muhammad as the arrogant Black man who had stubbornly refused to join the military but was now being allowed to fight again. Among these people he was still hated, so he had to be careful. Private guards were assigned to stay in the cottage with him and his staff while he trained.

Every morning at dawn Muhammad rose to begin his roadwork — running several miles through the wooded area bordering the highway. Muhammad would run for about an hour then later go to the gym a few miles away to spar in the ring. He was following a rigorous training schedule: up at five o'clock, roadwork, sparring, then bed by ten o'clock.

Muhammad's three-and-a-half-year exile had taken its toll. His thin, high-cheekboned face had filled out, giving it a wide, heavy look. It was still a handsome face, but the sly boyish grin had been replaced by a determined, almost grim look. The eyes could still be mischievous, flashing with merriment when he sprung a joke. But now they were most often serious.

Muhammad's body had also filled out, and grown even flabby around the middle. The years of physical inactivity had done that, and now it was harder to take and keep the weight off. So Muhammad faithfully followed the demanding training schedule. He had to. At the age of twenty-eight, which is considered almost old for a boxer, he was preparing for his comeback.

Several days before the fight, Muhammad was abruptly awakened out of a deep sleep. He didn't know why he had awakened so suddenly. Outside, the dawn air was still — almost a deathly stillness. Inside, members of Muhammad's crew were sound asleep: his father snoring in one room, his brother Rahaman sleeping down the hall, his friend Bundini asleep on the couch in the living room. The guard had left for the night.

Muhammad woke Bundini. "Get the gas!" he said playfully to his friend. "Time to get the gas!" Getting the gas meant it was time for Muhammad to begin his roadwork.

Bundini sat up quickly, rubbing his eyes. "What you up to, Champ?" he said, laughing.

But Muhammad was already out on the porch, dancing and shadowboxing the dark air, sucking in its fresh sweetness. He felt wonderful. In a few days he would be back where he belonged — the ring. He danced off the porch, moving with his old grace through the grass, still shadowboxing.

"Go get 'em, Champ!" Bundini cried delightedly from the doorway. "Get 'em for old times sake, Champ! You can whip him! I know you can whip . . . !"

Bang! A shot rang through the trees — *wheee!* Muhammad stopped dead in his tracks and whirled around. The shot had come from behind him.

Bang! Another shot ripped the air, giving off a blast of light as it flew past Muhammad.

"Hit the ground, Champ!" Bundini shouted frantically. "Get *down!*"

Muhammad dropped to the ground, and began crawling toward the house. From behind him, through the air of the morning darkness, came the sound of voices.

"You Black dog!" came one voice.

"Get out of Georgia!" came another.

"You draft-dodging nigger!" came the third.

Muhammad reached the safety of the house, and the entire household was now up.

"What's going on?" said Muhammad's father.

"They tryin' to kill yo' son!" Bundini cried with tears in his eyes. "They wanna stop the fight!"

Muhammad tried to phone the police, but the line was dead. Bundini suddenly darted to his couch and pulled out a case from underneath it. In it were two Colt .45s, which he quickly loaded; then he ran outside, waving both guns.

"Come on, if you wanna die!" he screamed from the porch as he fired the pistols. "Come *on!* We're ready for you!"

But the only response to Bundini's challenge was silence — deadly, still, and total silence. He went back in the house where the others were crouched, waiting expectantly.

Suddenly, the phone rang. One of Muhammad's staff picked it up, and then passed it to Muhammad. "It's for you," he said.

"Nigger! If you don't leave Atlanta tomorrow, you gonna die!" the voice on the other end ranted. "You Viet Cong nigger! You draft-dodging punk! We won't miss you next time! There ain't gonna be no fight in Atlanta!"

Muhammad hung up, but the phone rang again. More threats came from the other end, and then the person hung up.

"Try the police," Rahaman urged. But when Muhammad picked up the phone, it was once again dead.

There was nothing to do now but wait. In another hour it would be light. As he waited, Muhammad realized that this fight would have to take place. Whether or not he won the fight was beside the point. What mattered was that he fight again. For in fighting he would be scoring a victory over the thousands of hateful, spiteful people who would rather see him dead than be allowed to continue as a boxer.

If he fought again, he would be living proof that truth and order can be triumphant over ignorance and injustice.

Later, Muhammad's thoughts were interrupted by the sound of a car horn. A lieutenant from Atlanta's police department had driven up. He had two assistants with him, both heavily armed. They had come to escort Muhammad on his roadwork.

"We've gotten reports that there might be an attempt on your life," the lieutenant explained to Muhammad. "So we're providing you with extra security. Both here and at the gym."

Muhammad glanced quickly at his staff. He had told them not to say anything about the shooting incident. He was determined that *nothing* was going to stop this fight.

From the moment Muhammad had been told he was being allowed to fight in Atlanta, he had had a sinking feeling that something was going to happen to prevent it. To begin with, the state governor, Lester Maddox, was opposed. Although he could not legally stop it, Maddox proclaimed the fight date "a day of mourning for Atlanta," and urged people to boycott it.

Also, in New York, where Muhammad's lawyers were working to get his license restored, Governor Nelson Rockefeller refused to assist. He was afraid of angering President Richard Nixon if he granted Muhammad a license (which he had the power to do as governor). It was common knowledge in political circles that President Nixon *despised* Muhammad.

Given the number of powerful people who were opposed to Muhammad fighting again, it was no wonder that he worried. But there was also an even greater number of people who supported him. While he was in training in Atlanta, he received telephone calls from such personalities as Marlon Brando, Henry Fonda, and Diana Ross — all wishing him luck with his comeback match.

A group of Black promoters, headed by Senator Johnson, had guaranteed Muhammad a purse of over half a million dollars for his fight. Tickets to the fight in Atlanta's Auditorium were sold out. So were the tickets to the closed-circuit TV theaters on the East Coast. Russia, England, Germany, and Japan were beaming the fight in by satellite. Everybody, it seemed, wanted to see this fight — even many of those who were against it.

Muhammad's greatest support was coming from the very people who were hurrying to purchase tickets — ordinary people, neither rich nor famous, who saw Muhammad as fighting for them. As the young civil rights leader and minister Jesse Jackson said: "Whether he wants to or not, Jerry Quarry represents the Establishment. This fight is about democracy and how it is practiced by people like Lester Maddox, Spiro Agnew, George Wallace, Richard Nixon, on one hand, and by ordinary people, Black and white, on the other."

Jackson felt it was appropriate that the fight was being held in Atlanta, the hometown of the great Black leader Dr. Martin Luther King, Jr., who had been slain two years before. "Dr. King would have loved it this way," Jackson said.

Jerry Quarry was the leading contender for the heavyweight title, now held by Joe Frazier. Frazier had once knocked out Quarry, and Quarry had once lost the World Boxing Association's Elimination Tournament to Jimmy Ellis. Muhammad, on the other hand, had never lost a professional fight. And although he would be coming back from a three-year layoff, psychologically he had the edge over Quarry since he had never been defeated.

But Muhammad could not muster up the same old antagonism for Quarry as he had for men such as Sonny Liston and Floyd Patterson. Quarry was a tall, attractive boxer who seemed to hold the same admiration for Muhammad as did the majority of the public. He may have been viewed as the "Great White Hope" by those who still despised Muhammad, but Quarry had no personal grudge against Ali. Like most boxers, he was in the fight for profits, not politics.

Muhammad actually liked Quarry when the two first met to sign the contract several weeks before the fight. Quarry had brought his family along to the contract-signing ceremony, and his son, Jerry Lynn, was anxious to meet Muhammad.

"Mr. Ali, may I please have your autograph?" Jerry Lynn shyly asked Muhammad after being introduced.

Muhammad put his arm around the little boy, who had taken hold of his hand, and the two of them moved to a corner of the room, away from the crowd of questioning reporters. Muhammad has always loved children, and he is perhaps never more conscious of the brutality of boxing as when he meets an opponent's child. Frequently, after a fight, the first thing Muhammad would do was find the family of the opponent he had just defeated to assure them that he had not hurt their loved one too badly. Now, standing in the corner of the room, looking down at Quarry's son, Muhammad felt the old familiar mixture of pain and sadness. He signed his name right on the little boy's hand, then picked him up and held him in his arms. *How can I work up any hatred toward the father of this little boy?* he wondered to himself.

Like most boxers, Muhammad does not really deeply hate any of his opponents. He only *pretends* to hate them, since hatred helps to motivate the fighting. In some instances he may actually dislike an opponent, which makes the motivation come more easily. In other cases, such as leading up to his fight with Quarry, it has seemed impossible for Muhammad even to pretend hatred. But his feelings toward Quarry were to change, although Muhammad did not yet know it.

As the date of the fight approached, excitement and tension mounted rapidly. People from all over the country were flocking into the city of Atlanta to witness the comeback of Muhammad Ali.

The rich were coming, by plane or chauffeur-driven limousine. The not-so-rich were coming, by plane or train or bus, or driving themselves. The pimps and the hustlers were coming, also driven by chauffeurs, in long, sleek, Eldorado Cadillacs, Rolls-Royces, and Mercedes Benzes. The movie stars and the politicians were coming, by jets, with personal hairdressers and Secret Service men. The flower children were coming, by foot or on motorcycles or hitchhiking.

They were all coming — the men and women, the rich and the poor, the Black and the white — all united by a common hero: Muhammad Ali. As they converged on the city, the atmosphere became charged with the electrifying excitement which precedes a momentous event. But the Muhammad Ali–Jerry Quarry fight was to be more than just an event; it was to be a happening — a glittering, dazzling sports spectacular unequaled by any other event in boxing history.

The night before the fight, Muhammad himself descended upon the city. He had broken his ten o'clock curfew to be among his true fans, the people.

It was midnight, and he was leading a wild, cheering crowd through the quiet downtown streets of Atlanta.

"That's right!" he shouted to the crowd. "The real champ is gonna show the world who's the greatest! So get to the fight early." He leaped up on his toes, and started shadowboxing. "I'm feeling better than ever!" he screamed. "Better than ever!"

He moved quickly through the street, feinting, twostepping, doing his Ali shuffle, leading the crowd toward the Regency-Hyatt House Hotel, the headquarters of Jerry Quarry.

"Here I am!" he roared, bursting through the hotel door. The lobby was jammed with people waiting for just this moment — waiting to see Ali, *their* champion, come gliding through the door. A piercing cheer went up. "Aleeee!"

"Here I am!" Muhammad shouted again. "The king is *here!*" Deafening applause greeted that statement, followed by some clenched, raised fists. The king was *back*.

October 26, 1970. The long-awaited day of the Muhammad Ali–Jerry Quarry fight had finally arrived. In a few hours Muhammad would end his more-than-three-year exile. But now he was going through the prefight weigh-in ceremony.

For this weigh-in, bleachers had been built to accommodate the hundreds of people who were crowded in the room to see Muhammad. He stripped to trunks first, and slowly proceeded through the pushing crowd up to the scales.

Suddenly, Muhammad heard a commotion coming from the other side of the room — the side where Jerry Quarry was making his entrance. Muhammad spotted Quarry, and saw that his face was red and contorted as if he were trying to keep it from exploding. He was screaming something, but Muhammad could not make out what it was. But as Quarry got closer, Muhammad heard him loud and clear.

"I ain't gettin' in the ring with no Black doctors in my corner!" Quarry was screaming. "If that's what I gotta do, the fight's off!"

Muhammad then noticed, for the first time, that the two doctors sent by the Atlanta State Commission to conduct the physicals at the weigh-in, and to serve as house physicians for the fight, were both Black.

Muhammad was amazed. Quarry was making all this fuss about having two Black doctors at the fight? In all of his years of fighting, the doctors assigned to Muhammad's fights were always white, and he had never even *thought* of complaining, even though most boxers are Black or Latin.

"Well, well, well!" Muhammad shouted over the noise Quarry was making. "We got *soul* doctors in the house for once! Welcome, brothers, welcome!" Muhammad began to clap his hands in applause, and soon everyone in the room joined in.

Quarry was still enraged at the prospect of the two Black doctors, but was beginning to calm down.

"What's going on?" Muhammad asked his trainer, Angelo Dundee, after spotting several men whispering to Quarry.

"They told him he wouldn't have to accept Black doctors," Dundee said. "Quarry thinks a Black doctor might find some excuse for stopping the fight and awarding the decision to you."

Now it was Muhammad's turn to get angry. Did Quarry really think Muhammad would need the help of a doctor to beat him? Muhammad took a good, hard look at Quarry at that moment, and began to see him for what he really was — an arrogant racist. "Quarry is the one who's going to be screaming for the help of a doctor by the time I get through with him," Muhammad said under his breath. "A doctor of *any* color!"

After the two men were given their physicals, they were asked to pose together for pictures. Muhammad took this opportunity to inform Quarry of what he could expect later that night in the ring.

"You're gonna get the worst damn whipping of your life," he whispered viciously in Quarry's ear. "I'm gonna whip you till you're cherry red. You insulted those Black doctors!"

Quarry tried to pull away, but Muhammad went on, relentlessly. "If you don't want Black doctors who are here to *help* you, how you must hate Black me, who's here to *hurt* you," he said. "And hurt you I will!"

Quarry looked upset, as if a blow had already struck his face. Muhammad knew he had gotten to him. As with most of his previous opponents, who had fallen victim to Muhammad's mouth during the weigh-in, Quarry was already beaten — it was now simply a matter of finishing him off in the ring that night.

Or was it? Although the two doctors had pronounced Muhammad physically fit for the fight, questions still haunted him, questions he knew others were continuing to ask each other, but never him directly.

"Isn't he pretty old to be making a comeback?"

"Do you think he still has the speed?"

"Does he really expect to be champion again, after all those years of inactivity?"

Muhammad was also asking himself these questions. Just before the fight he admitted to former champion Joe Louis that he was nervous. A comeback for Muhammad didn't just mean fighting again, it meant recapturing the world heavyweight crown, and he knew that was a long shot. The only heavyweight champion to lose his crown and then win it back had been Floyd Patterson, first losing to, then defeating, the Swede Ingemar Johansson. Patterson, however, had not been out of action for three years the way Muhammad had.

These were some of the thoughts spinning through Muhammad's head as the clock moved toward his appointed hour with Jerry Quarry, and fight fans assembled at Atlanta's Civic Auditorium to witness "The Comeback."

Outside the auditorium it looked as if the event inside was going to be a gala costume ball rather than a ferocious boxing match. Fans arrived who clearly had come to see the fight and to *be seen.* There were women in long flowing evening gowns. There were pimps dressed in mink and diamonds, with their women dressed in revealing miniskirts. There were farmers in jeans and overalls. There were city slickers in gold lamé jumpsuits and white three-piece suits with matching wide-brim hats.

Inside the mood was festive. The champ was back and there was going to be partying tonight. The stars had come out to celebrate. Sitting ringside, near Muhammad's corner, was Diana Ross, draped in fur. Seated in the press area was Bill Cosby. Behind the press area but also sitting ringside were Sidney Poitier, The Supremes, Whitney Young, Julian Bond, Hank Aaron, Mrs. Martin Luther King, Jr.

It was an all-star Black crowd, come to shine on the brightest star of all — Muhammad Ali.

Curtis Mayfield sang the "Star-Spangled Banner" in his own sultry, soulful style. The audience then sat through the preliminary fight, anxiously waiting for the Quarry-Ali bout.

The preliminary fight ended. Suddenly, there came a burst of noise from the back of the auditorium. The crowd turned and saw Jerry Quarry nervously making his way toward the ring. There was mild applause as Quarry got in the ring and went to his corner.

Then there was another rush of noise, this time louder and more intense. The crowd looked again, and then suddenly leaped to its feet, shouting, and stomping and screaming for the man who was making his entrance.

"Aleeeee! Aleeeee! *Aleeeee!*" the crowd roared. The cry went up like a plaintive wail, echoing in the auditorium, the city, the world. Muhammad Ali was returning, and the people were jubilant.

"Aleee! . . . Aleee! . . . ," they continued to wail, some standing with tears in their eyes.

Muhammad moved gracefully through the crowd, shadowboxing, feeling a renewed surge of energy with each new cheer coming up from the people. He stepped in the ring and the crowd went completely wild, screaming with an intensity that bordered on hysteria. Muhammad did a few steps of his Ali shuffle before going to his corner, arms already waved in victory.

The bell rang for round one. Muhammad threw the first punch, a hard left jab that landed squarely in Quarry's face. Quarry was stunned. Muhammad threw two more jabs, quick ones, then a straight right cross. All of his blows neatly hit their mark.

Quarry was trying to move out of the way, but Muhammad kept pursuing. Finally, Quarry threw a punch, a bad left hook that missed Muhammad by a foot. Muhammad threw a flurry of punches, all on target. He was in complete control of the round, with Quarry trying unsuccessfully to get out of his way.

During round two, Muhammad slowed down a little, as if he were trying to conserve some of his strength. Quarry began to take the offensive. He threw a hook and a straight right, both of which hit Muhammad. Quarry threw two

Muhammad, on the comeback trail, defeats Jerry Quarry in Atlanta in 1970.

more hooks, but they were blocked by Muhammad. But Muhammad was now moving back, followed by Quarry, who threw a powerful left hook straight to Muhammad's body. Muhammad leaned against the ropes, leaving himself open to more attacks from Quarry. The bell sounded, ending the round.

The crowd murmured. This was going to be an exciting fight! In the first two rounds, it looked as if Muhammad had won the first round, and Quarry had won the second.

The bell sounded for round three. Muhammad came

out slowly. But Quarry was alert. He threw a right that landed on Muhammad's body. Muhammad threw two punches, but neither of them connected. Muhammad was now up on his toes, moving, making Quarry follow. Muhammad threw a short left jab that hit, then the two fighters were close together, throwing short punches. Then they broke; Muhammad moved in. He threw a flurry of punches, all making contact. Blood covered Quarry's face and he looked badly cut. The bell sounded.

When the bell rang for round four, Quarry did not come out. The cut over his eye was too deep for him to continue, and the referee ruled the fight over. Quarry was outraged. Why? Why? his expression seemed to ask. Tears were rolling down his cheeks.

But the crowd was ignoring Quarry's tears, as it screamed in triumph. Muhammad Ali had won the fight! Muhammad raised his arms in victory. His friend Bundini rushed over to hug him. The crowd roared until it seemed it would roar forever. Their champ not only was back, but he was back a winner! He was back with a vengeance! He was back to regain the crown!

"Aleeeee! Aleeeee!" the people screamed with total, unrestrained joy.

8
Going Down for the First Time

> Joe's gonna come out smokin',
> And I ain't gonna be jokin',
> I'll be peckin; and pokin',
> Pourin' water on his smokin'.
> This might shock and amaze ya,
> But I'll retire Joe Frazier!
> — *Muhammad Ali*

The fighter who becomes world heavyweight champion is said to be wearing the heavyweight "crown." Like the lion in the jungle, he is the king — the one who defeated all contenders and emerged from the pack victorious; rated the biggest and the strongest and the best. He looms above all the others, seated on the throne of success.

Yet the throne can also be a lonely seat. Although a champion is constantly surrounded by people — beautiful women, adoring crowds, other celebrities — he seldom has any real friends among other heavyweight fighters. He knows that only one man can wear the crown and that the fighter he calls his buddy may also be the next fighter trying to capture the crown by destroying him in the ring.

So, like the lion, the heavyweight champion is often

forced to roam the jungle alone, always surveying the territory, ever alert to the next attack, which may knock him off the throne.

Muhammad felt that if any heavyweight fighter could be his friend it was Joe Frazier. Joe was one of the "new breed" of boxers — not as outspoken or controversial as Muhammad, but definitely his own man. He was most often called "Smokin' Joe" because he had a massive body that was built like a tank and moved like a steamroller; he was steady and deadly, driven by an inexhaustible iron will.

Beneath the fierce exterior, however, "Smokin' Joe" was also gentle Joe, a quiet, soft-spoken man whose sparkling eyes and brilliant smile could light up a room. He was in the boxing business simply because the business was good to him. As a boxer he could make more money in a single fight than he could make in a year at the slaughterhouse he had worked at in Philadelphia.

Like most boxers, Frazier had come up the hard way. He was the youngest of thirteen children born on a small farm in Beaufort, North Carolina. His father had lost his left arm in an accident, and many people believed Frazier had developed his powerful left hook punch to compensate for the loss of his father's arm.

Frazier started boxing when he was six, inspired by Joe Louis, who had just become heavyweight champion. At the age of fourteen, Frazier quit school and moved to New York to find work. A year later he moved to Philadelphia, where he worked cutting meat in a slaughterhouse. In spite of his hard work, Frazier began to get fat, so he started boxing at a gym to get back in shape.

He was a slow and awkward fighter, but had fierce determination and incredible strength. A trainer at the gym named Yank Durham spotted Frazier and began giving him lessons. Under Durham's guidance, Joe perfected his fighting style, which consisted of a nonstop charging attack, combined with powerful punches. His astonishing strength enabled him to take blows while he wore an opponent down with his own steady barrage of punches.

In 1964, Frazier won the Gold Medal in boxing at the Olympics, and a few months later he decided to turn professional. He scored impressive victories within a few years — the same years during which Muhammad was languishing in exile. In 1970 Joe defeated Jimmy Ellis, the World Boxing Association's recognized heavyweight champion. Joe was now considered the legitimate world heavyweight champion.

It was also in 1970 that Muhammad Ali and Joe Frazier met and talked together as potential friends. Muhammad was still in exile and had been working on his autobiography. He wanted to include Joe in it. He also wanted to get to know Joe better. He admired and respected Frazier, and despite all the odds against it, Muhammad felt it was possible for the two men to be buddies.

So, on a hot day in August of 1970, the two fighters got together — one the officially recognized heavyweight champion, the other the unofficially recognized heavyweight champion, both of them undefeated fighters.

Frazier was driving the two of them to New York from Philadelphia, and Muhammad was taping the conversation. They talked of many things: what Joe could expect to earn now that he was heavyweight champion, how the two men kept their weight down, how Joe's rock band was coming, which one of them had the better singing voice.

"You ever heard me sing?" Muhammad asked. "What you think of my singing?"

"You can't sing a little bit, man," Joe responded with a grin.

"I was a hit on Broadway!" Muhammad said indignantly. "You never heard my 'Mighty White' song?"

"Sheeeeiiiit!" Frazier said, totally unimpressed.

Then the two men sang a song together, and as their voices blended in harmony, each looked at the other with respect.

As they drove into New York, people on the street who recognized them were shocked. "What the hell are you two doing together?" asked a man who spotted them and ran over to the car.

"We're going to get it on in the alley!" Muhammad shouted, and he and Frazier laughed.

But the laughter was strained. They both knew that if Muhammad were allowed to fight again, they would have to meet each other in the ring. They had talked about it during the drive up.

"Tell the truth, now, man," Muhammad had said teasingly. "If you fought me, wouldn't you be scared?"

"No, man. Honest to God," Frazier answered quickly.

"You really wouldn't be scared?"

"No kinda way!"

When Frazier dropped Muhammad off in New York, people in the street recognized him immediately and came rushing over.

"Hey, Champ! Wait up, Champ!" several people called to Muhammad, wanting his autograph. They hadn't recognized Frazier, who was parked at the curb, watching the commotion around Muhammad.

"When you going to fight again, Champ?" someone asked.

"You're still the best in my book, Champ," said another.

"How about the fight with Frazier?" someone else asked. "You think you can beat Frazier?"

Muhammad told the crowd to ask Frazier himself, who was still sitting in the car. But the crowd ignored the man in the car, refusing to believe it was really Joe Frazier.

A feeling of sadness began creeping over Muhammad as the crowd continued to surround him, asking for his autograph and throwing out questions about Frazier. He suddenly realized that he and Frazier could not be friends. As long as the two men remained undefeated, there would always be confusion over which one of them was the real champion. At some point they would have to meet face-to-face in the ring to settle that question.

Muhammad looked up from the autographs he was signing and saw that Joe had gotten out of the car and was standing with his arms folded, watching him.

Frazier, at that moment, had the look of a shrewd hunter, a hunter stalking his prey, sizing him up, trying to locate the most vulnerable spot to move on for the kill. Muhammad felt a chill shoot through him. A few minutes ago, he and Frazier had been on the verge of becoming buddies. That prospect was gone now. Despite what the World Boxing Association said, Joe knew he would never be considered heavyweight champion by the *people* until he defeated Muhammad Ali. He nodded to Muhammad, who understood that, too; then he got back in his car and sped away.

The Muhammad Ali–Joe Frazier day of reckoning was to come sooner than either man expected. Shortly after their drive together up to New York, Muhammad was allowed to fight Jerry Quarry in Atlanta. His victory over Quarry brought Muhammad one man closer to a title fight with Frazier.

That man was Oscar Bonavena, a tough Argentinian, whom Muhammad fought two months after beating Quarry. Muhammad defeated Bonavena, but it had been a rough fight. He had gone the entire fifteen rounds and received several grueling punches before knocking Bonavena out. Muhammad was not as fast on his feet as he had been before his three-year exile, and it showed during the Bonavena match.

Nevertheless, he won, and the way was now cleared for

the big fight and the big prize — Joe Frazier and the heavyweight championship.

Even while Muhammad was still in exile, there had been talk of a match between him and Joe Frazier. Both Muhammad and Joe were enormously popular among different segments of the public: Muhammad appealing to the more radical and militant young people who were seeking to change the system; Joe appealing to the more conservative Blacks and whites who liked his humble, unassuming manner and the fact that he minded his own business and didn't make waves.

Promoters were certain that a Muhammad Ali–Joe Frazier match would draw from both these segments of the public and could possibly be the biggest moneymaker ever in the sport of boxing. They had already glimpsed the powerful potential of an Ali-Frazier fight during Muhammad's exile, when he staged a phony fight with Frazier.

At that time Muhammad knew that if he could show he was still an exciting crowd pleaser, capable of attracting people and money to his fights, he might be allowed to fight again. He got an idea, and called Frazier about it.

"Listen, Joe, I'm gonna call the newspapers and radio stations and tell them you dared me to a fight. I'm gonna tell 'em I'm coming over to your gym at four o'clock, to decide once and for all who's the real champion, you dig?"

Joe understood, and agreed immediately. He, too, recognized that if Muhammad were allowed to fight again, it would mean big money for both of them if they had a real fight.

Muhammad hung up, and quickly began calling the news media with the story. After he finished, his own phone started ringing with calls from reporters who wanted to know what was happening.

"You really fighting Frazier in his gym?" one of them asked.

"Yes!" Muhammad shouted. "You caught me just in time. I'm on my way out the door now. See you at the gym!"

Muhammad had no intention of having a real fight with Frazier, but he knew the prospect of a possible fight would attract attention — particularly from promoters. He went out to get in his car and saw that a mob of photographers had already gathered in front of the house, waiting to snap pictures of the ex-champion going to try to snatch the crown from Frazier.

In the car Muhammad listened with delight to his radio broadcasting news of the fight.

"This is the big Philadelphia showdown, folks!" he cried out the window to people as his car roared down the street. "The great fight has come to Philly! Free! It'll all be free if you get there early!"

People everywhere dropped what they were doing and nearly stampeded over to the gym. Some were speeding in cars to get there, others were running on foot.

There were so many people that when Muhammad got about ten blocks from the gym, he found it was impossible to get through by car. He walked the rest of the way, and the crowd grew even larger.

"Ali's going to meet Frazier!" someone from a window shouted.

"A fight! A fight! A fight!" the crowd chanted.

Muhammad reached the gym, surrounded by a howling crowd. "Where's Joe Frazier?" he shouted, banging on the door. "Open up, Joe, and face me like a man!"

The door opened and the crowd pushed Muhammad in. "I'm sick and tired of hearing people say Frazier is the champion!" Muhammad screamed, taking off his jacket. "There can't be two champions! Let's settle this right now, once and for all!"

But there were too many people jammed in the gym to have the fight there. A policeman suggested they fight in a nearby park.

"To the park!" Muhammad suddenly yelled, leading the people back outside. "We're gonna get it on in the park!"

Frazier, however, did not show up at the park. His managers had convinced him to wait until he could fight Muhammad legally, and for money.

Muhammad didn't mind. He had made his point, and Frazier had helped him to make it. He was still the most exciting crowd draw in boxing. Over 20,000 people had come to the park to witness the "fight."

He and Frazier signed a real fight contract in December, 1970, and the match was set for March 8 of the next year in New York's Madison Square Garden. The publicity and promotions surrounding the forthcoming event were filled with even more razzle-dazzle hype than Muhammad himself could dream up.

First there was the purse. Both Muhammad and Frazier were being guaranteed two and a half million dollars for the match, regardless of who won or lost! It was the largest sum paid to boxers in the history of the game.

Next, the fight was being billed as "The Battle of the Century" — the final showdown between two undefeated fighters representing opposite poles of American thought. Joe Frazier was being hailed as yet another "Great White Hope," doing battle against that troublesome nigger, Muhammad Ali.

The fact that the two men actually were more similar than different only made promoters and sportswriters more determined to emphasize their differences. Contrast was what sold tickets.

Muhammad and Joe began to emphasize their differences to each other, too, and soon it became difficult to tell when they were kidding and when they were serious.

Muhammad would accuse Joe of being an "Uncle Tom," because he was managed by a group of white men and was the favored fighter of the Establishment.

Joe would accuse Muhammad of being a "phony," pointing out that although Muhammad "talked Black," he had a white trainer.

Muhammad contended that Frazier was a "slugger," and not a boxer with any real style or grace. "If Frazier beats me, I'll crawl across the ring on my hands and knees and tell him he's the greatest," he bragged. "He's gonna be so outclassed that it'll be no contest. *No contest!*"

The excitement that grew over this fight was surpassing even Muhammad's comeback fight. Tickets sold out almost the instant they went on sale at Madison Square Garden. They ranged in price from $20 to $150 — the most ever charged by the Garden. Some ticket buyers, more interested in money than the match, "scalped" their tickets by selling them to others for outrageous prices. A ringside seat went for $1,500 from scalpers. More enterprising scalpers even made counterfeit tickets, which were sold to unsuspecting buyers.

Yet, some were willing to pay any price to witness the event. A rich Texas oil man tried to get five tickets for $5,000; another fan offered to pay $20,000 for twenty seats.

The promoters were predicting a million-dollar gate at the Garden, and were expecting to bring in about twenty million dollars more from closed-circuit television theaters around the world. The fight was to be shown in 337 theaters in the United States and Canada and 46 countries in Europe, South America, Africa, the Far East, and Australia. Over thirty million people would be watching!

Muhammad Ali was unquestionably the most exciting personality the world had ever seen. His popularity exceeded that of kings, presidents, the Pope, and rock stars.

It was a stunning achievement for a man who had begun his career as the unfavored underdog, first dismissed, then despised. Even among those who still hated him, he commanded respect and awe.

Shortly before the date of the fight, Muhammad predicted that he would defeat Frazier by the sixth round. Frazier's trainer, Yank Durham, made a prediction of his own — "Frazier'll take Ali out by round ten."

Frazier was actually the one favored to win. Boxing experts who had seen Muhammad's last fight against Oscar Bonavena knew the former champ had lost some of his former speed. They didn't think he would be able to stand up under, or get away from, Frazier's grinding pressure and devastating punches.

But Muhammad, as usual, did not seem worried. He was training in Miami, and would entertain the throngs of people who dropped by the camp with wonderful tales of how he was going to demolish Frazier in the ring.

"I'll glide in an' out, in an' out, pop, pop, pop!" he said merrily. The crowds loved him, and Muhammad loved the crowds. They were his strength.

Frazier, on the other hand, was training up in the Catskill mountain area of New York in quiet seclusion. He avoided crowds. They interfered with his concentration. In the evenings, he often entertained himself by strumming his guitar and singing a few rock tunes. He had formed a rock band about a year before, called the Knockouts, and wanted to keep his voice in shape as well as his body.

Still representing different images to their fans, Frazier and Ali were both deadly opponents — gladiators, preparing to do battle in the public arena of judgment. Only one could emerge victorious, and he would stand alone, recognized by the world as the rightful heir to the heavyweight championship crown.

On the day of the fight, the weigh-ins were held separately, since officials were afraid that Muhammad and Frazier would try to tear each other apart if they were in the same room together. As a joke, someone suggested that, along with the fighters' other measurements, their mouths be measured also. Muhammad and Frazier agreed. The results were not surprising.

Frazier's mouth measured five inches closed and eight and a half inches open. Muhammad's mouth was six inches closed and eleven inches open. He would always win that contest!

On the night of the fight, the area around Madison Square Garden looked as if half the population of New York City had gathered on that one spot. Traffic was jammed for blocks as herds of people flocked around the Garden, some trying to get inside, some trying to catch a glimpse of the fighters, some ogling the people going inside, and still others trying to hustle. These were the pickpockets, the pimps, the prostitutes, and the scalpers.

Many of those who had tickets were forced to wait as long as an hour before they could get in. Those trying to buy tickets from the scalpers were haggling over prices. One woman had her ticket snatched out of her hand as she presented it to the attendant. The thief darted through the crowd, and immediately tried to sell it to someone else!

Inside, the Garden was packed with 20,525 people. It was a record attendance for an indoor sporting event. The total amount taken in from the sale of tickets was $1,352,951 — another record.

Seated in the audience was a celebrities' gallery of such notables as Ethel Kennedy, the composer Burt Bacharach, singer Nancy Wilson, Senator Hubert Humphrey, mayor of New York John V. Lindsay, former light-heavyweight champion José Torres. This was to be a grand night, indeed!

A mighty roar went up in the Garden when Muhammad entered. Since he was the challenger, he was required to enter first.

"Champ! Champ! Champ!" the crowd screamed. Muhammad looked magnificent in red velvet boxing trunks and white shoes with red tassels on the laces. He waved confidently.

Then Frazier entered and another howling roar went up.

"Joe! Joe! *Jooooeeee!*" his fans shrieked. He was splendid in green and gold brocade boxing trunks. He also waved.

The crowd began to settle down, waiting expectantly for the bell to sound.

Up in the ring the referee was giving final instructions to the two fighters. He finished, and Muhammad and Frazier moved back to their respective corners to wait.

The bell rang: round one. Frazier came out quickly, heading straight for Muhammad. Muhammad circled around him, but Frazier kept coming and suddenly threw a short jab that connected. Muhammad felt it — a dull pain. He struck back, and then began shooting left jabs at Frazier's head. But Frazier was escaping most of them. He continued to come at Muhammad, swinging, letting lose a torrent of punches against Ali's body. The two fighters went into a clinch, and for the first time, Muhammad felt the real strength of Frazier's body. It was like hot steel. Frazier kept up his attack.

People began to scream, "Joe! Joe! Come on, Joe!" Frazier was clearly winning this first round.

During rounds two and three, Muhammad managed to get back some control of the fight. But in the middle of round four, Frazier threw his famous left hook. It hit Muhammad square in the jaw with a force so great that to Ali it felt like an explosion.

Muhammad started circling Frazier during round five, but Frazier kept coming in, harder, faster, throwing punches at the body. Muhammad threw a sharp uppercut that snapped Frazier's head back. But he kept coming, unmercifully, tirelessly. Muhammad wondered how much longer either of them could keep up the pace. Frazier looked as if he would never stop. Muhammad began to have a new respect for him.

Frazier came out hard and fast during round six. He knew this was the round in which Muhammad had predicted he would knock him out, and he wanted to establish himself clearly as the one in control. Muhammad shot straight jabs at him, but Frazier began backing him into a corner. Muhammad lay back on the ropes, and Frazier threw a steady barrage of left hooks to his hips and ribs. Then he moved the punches up toward the head, and Muhammad began to feel a pain so intense he thought his whole body would go numb. Frazier continued his smashing attacks, his short, massive arms striking his target with awesome power.

The audience was beside itself, smelling the scent of defeat. The people began to scream for the blood of Muhammad. "Joe! Joe! Come on! Finish him!"

Muhammad was weak. It was as though all of his physical and spiritual forces had suddenly abandoned him. He was getting the beating of his life.

He recovered some of his strength during the seventh round, and held Frazier off. But during round eight, Frazier came on again, smoking, delivering his brutal blows. The crowd started booing Muhammad. "Take him out, Joe!" the people demanded. "Take him *out!*"

Muhammad had another surge of strength during round nine, and he threw straight rights to Frazier's head that were connecting. Frazier started backing off and Muhammad threw more punches. Frazier's nose was bleeding; there was a huge lump over his eye. At the end of the round, Frazier was bleeding all over — from over his eye, from his nose and his mouth. But he wasn't going to stop. And Muhammad realized, in a flash, that the only way to stop Joe Frazier now would be to kill him.

Frazier tried to take Muhammad out during round ten, the round his own trainer predicted he would win. He was

Muhammad goes down for the first time in his Madison Square Garden fight with Joe Frazier in 1971. (CAMERA 5, KEN REGAN)

all over Muhammad, bombarding him with his shattering left hook. Muhammad felt the weariness return. He had five more rounds to go, and wasn't sure if he could make it.

During the eleventh, twelfth, and thirteenth rounds Frazier came on ferociously. His face was a bloody mess, but his body was still smoking, plunging onward, out to destroy Muhammad Ali.

Frazier was beginning to get to Muhammad psychologically. He had never fought anyone with the sheer will and determination of this man. For the first time in his boxing career, Muhammad was actually frightened. He had an idea that in a few minutes he was going to know what it felt like to lose.

Now it was just a matter of getting through the last two rounds. He managed the fourteenth round. But during round fifteen, the crowd began its final cry for Muhammad's defeat.

"Come on, Joe! Knock him out! Kill him!"

Frazier, perhaps inspired by the cries of the audience, suddenly bent over in a half-stooped position and then quickly leaped up with his left fist headed straight for Muhammad's head. Muhammad saw the hook coming, but before he could react the punch landed. He felt himself slowly ... slowly ... slipping into darkness.

Muhammad fell to the floor of the ring. It wasn't until he heard the roar of the people blasting in his ear that he realized Frazier had just knocked him down! He got up, but the roar from the crowd was even greater.

He and Frazier finished the round, and when the bell rang, Muhammad went to his corner already aware of what the judges' decision would be.

"The winner by unanimous decision," shouted the announcer over the microphone, "the undisputed world heavyweight champion — Joe Frazier!"

The people in the Garden went crazy. They screamed and cheered and began rushing toward the ring trying to get to both Frazier and Muhammad.

Frazier made his way through the crowd over to Muhammad's corner. "You put up a great fight," he said to Muhammad, shaking his hand.

"You the champ," Muhammad said quietly. He remembered he had promised he would crawl across the ring to Frazier if Frazier won this fight and tell him he was the greatest.

Frazier remembered that too, but he said to Muhammad softly, "We don't do no crawling. You fought one helluva fight. We both the greatest, and we don't do no crawling."

People were suddenly pushing by Muhammad trying to get to shake hands with Joe Frazier, the champion.

For many people, though, Muhammad was still the *real* champion, despite his loss. He had fought his greatest match in the ring of public opinion and the arena of the American courts — and won.

On June 21, 1971, three months after his defeat by Joe Frazier, Muhammad Ali's draft evasion sentence was overthrown by the United States Supreme Court. He was cleared of all charges.

So, although Muhammad Ali was a weary and bruised man when he retreated to his dressing room that night after losing to Joe Frazier, he was also undisputedly a winner.

Later that night, after all the crowds had gone, someone scrawled on the wall of a Harlem subway station in big, bold, defiant letters: "Ali Lives!"

9
After the Fall, the Rise

The butterfly has lost its wings,
The bee has lost its sting.
— *Anonymous hate letter
sent to Muhammad Ali*

"I guess I ain't pretty no more," Muhammad wearily told the mob of reporters who had invaded his dressing room right after his defeat by Joe Frazier. He was stretched out on a rubbing table, holding his jaw, which had swollen up like a balloon from Frazier's battering left hook. Both of his eyes were blackened. He certainly was *not* a pretty sight.

"So, whatya gonna do now, Champ?" several reporters wanted to know. He was still a "champ" to them.

"Some people say your career is finished," another reporter said snidely. "They say this is the end of the line for you."

Muhammad was startled by this last comment. Of course, he had suffered a defeat. But he was not *crushed* by it. He wanted the reporters to know that — he wanted everyone to know. That was why he had let the reporters and television crews in his dressing room in the first place, over the strong objections of his trainers and close friends.

"They just want to film you and your swollen jaw so the whole world can see that you've been beaten!" Bundini cried, protesting the reporters' presence in the dressing room.

"So what?" Muhammad responded. "I've always let 'em in after a victory, so I'll let them see me after a defeat. I want the people who believe in me see that I'm not finished, that I've had a defeat just like they've had defeats. But I'll get up and come back again, just like other people do."

Muhammad was true to his word. A few days after the fight, he was up, and running off at the mouth — which was more than could be said for Joe Frazier. Unlike Muhammad, who had at least been able to *walk* away from the fight in defeat, Frazier had been on the verge of collapsing and was *carried* back to his dressing room after beating Muhammad. He was so bloodied and battered that he had to spend the next six weeks in the hospital recovering from his "victory."

Muhammad, on the other hand, appeared on the Howard Cosell sports show the next Saturday (he and Frazier had both been supposed to appear), already his old self, proclaiming himself still the champion.

"I'm the people's champion," he said simply. "And I truly believe I won that fight with Frazier. I know I outpointed him, but the judges' decision was against me, and I never argue with the judges' decision."

He did, however, insist on a return match with Frazier to prove his claim that he was the better fighter. "Them judges just didn't like my religion, nor my stand on the draft," he explained. "But it's clear I was the real winner. I mean, I was able to make it to this show and Frazier wasn't!"

Once again, Muhammad was making his pitch to the public, using the two instruments he played best — his mouth and the media. Muhammad knew that the power of his words increased in direct proportion to the number of people they reached. The most effective way to reach the greatest number of people was through the media — television, radio, newspapers, and magazines. Early in his career Muhammad had become skilled at using all of these vehicles whenever he wanted to make a point or attract attention. And it always worked. After all, Muhammad Ali was *news*.

Now, a week after losing to Joe Frazier, he was back in business, using the media to drum up enthusiasm and support and money for a second Joe Frazier fight.

It wasn't going to be simple, however. Frazier was reluctant to fight Muhammad a second time. Perhaps his six-week stay in the hospital had convinced him that Muhammad Ali was not an opponent to be taken lightly, that next time Muhammad might not only put him in the hospital, but might actually win the fight. So Frazier continued to stall. He wanted to enjoy his champion status for as long as possible.

Muhammad, meanwhile, fought a host of lesser opponents during the next two years. His first fight after his loss to Frazier was against Jimmy Ellis, his old sparring partner and hometown friend, who had also become the recognized champion during Muhammad's exile. Muhammad knocked Ellis out in the twelfth round of the fight, settling once and for all any questions as to which of them was the superior fighter.

He also fought both Jerry Quarry and Floyd Patterson and beat them, each for a second time. His fight with Patterson was actually undertaken as a favor to Floyd, who badly needed the money. The two men had never been friends, but over the years they had both become big enough to forget their differences. Muhammad remembered that Patterson, the same man who challenged him to a fight after his defeat over Liston, was also one of the few fighters who came to see his Broadway performance in *Buck White* during his exile. Muhammad had been very touched by Patterson's attendance that night.

During their second fight in 1972, Muhammad finished Patterson off quickly in the seventh round. He had no wish to humiliate Patterson the way he had a few years before, when the two men seemed to be basically fighting a holy war between Christianity and Islam.

By February of 1973, Muhammad had taken on ten fights since his defeat by Frazier and easily won them all. But he was still pressing for a second Joe Frazier fight. So were promoters. Muhammad and Frazier continued to be the two most popular figures in boxing, and promoters knew another fight between the two would once again bring in huge sums of money.

Yet, Frazier still refused. In fact, while Muhammad had fought ten times since the Frazier match, Frazier had defended his title only five times in championship matches. He seemed determined not only to wear the crown for as long as possible, but to fight as infrequently as possible.

In 1973, however, Frazier met his match when he took on a brutal boxer named George Foreman in a title fight in Kingston, Jamaica. Foreman, twenty-four years old, knocked Frazier down three times in the first round of the fight. During the second round, he floored him again three times, and the referee stopped the fight, declaring George Foreman the winner and the new world heavyweight champion.

The public was stunned. Muhammad was outraged. Frazier's defeat had cost them both another shot at a title fight and another large purse.

On March 31, 1973, two months after Frazier's loss to Foreman, Muhammad was scheduled to fight Frazier's old sparring partner — Ken Norton. Norton was not a highly rated fighter, and fans and sportswriters weren't giving him much of a chance against Muhammad.

Muhammad himself figured it would be another routine victory. Norton was said to be a slow-moving fighter who left himself wide open to attack and had only one good punch — a left hook.

Frazier felt otherwise. "Norton is a good fighter, very much underrated," he said with certainty. "I should know — I've sparred in the ring with him."

But little attention was being paid to Frazier's observations, or his predictions that Norton could win against Muhammad. Paying least attention of all was Muhammad himself, who was so confident of a victory over Norton that he didn't even bother to train as much as usual. He was actually in flabby shape.

The fight was scheduled to go twelve rounds and be held in San Diego, California, Norton's hometown. The night before the fight a party was held at Muhammad's hotel, and he spent most of the evening entertaining crowds of people, with antics showing how he intended to demolish Norton the following day. He was putting on his standard performance. There seemed no question that he would win.

On the day of the fight Muhammad weighed in considerably heavier than his usual 214 pounds. But it didn't seem to bother him that he was out of shape. Norton would be a pushover.

The fight was held at 2:30 in the afternoon of March 31, 1973. Sitting ringside was Joe Frazier, who had come to root for Norton.

The bell rang for round one. Muhammad and Norton moved out to the middle of the ring, but no punches were passed. Muhammad stood perfectly still, as if transfixed.

He had promised that during the fight he was going to pretend to hypnotize Norton. He knew Norton used a professional hypnotist to help him mentally prepare for his fights.

But it soon began to look as if Muhammad's hypnotist act wasn't working.

In the second round Muhammad once again did nothing. But Norton began throwing punches. They didn't appear particularly devastating, but he won the round.

Muhammad came out dancing during round three — moving all over the ring, staying out of Norton's reach. This was the round in which Muhammad had predicted he would knock Norton out. He didn't succeed at that, but he clearly won the round.

During round four, Muhammad went back to doing nothing, and Norton took that round.

Rounds five and six and seven came and went unspectacularly. In round eight, Muhammad's mouth looked strange — as if it were permanently twisted.

Rounds nine and ten were uneventful. Then in round eleven, Muhammad came out dancing the way he had in round three. He won the round.

During round twelve, the last one, Norton started throwing punches in earnest. He hit Muhammad back and forth across the ring, throwing several sharp punches straight to the left side of Muhammad's jaw. The blows landed hard and clean. Muhammad's head snapped back each time he was hit, and he looked badly hurt. The bell sounded, ending the fight.

The judges seemed to be taking forever to arrive at a decision. There was a flurry of activity around Muhammad. His doctor was examining him. His trainers looked worried.

Then came the judges' decision. The winner by a unanimous decision — Ken Norton! There followed an even more startling announcement: Ken Norton had broken Muhammad Ali's jaw during the fight! And he had broken it as early as round two of the match!

Pandemonium broke loose in the auditorium as thousands of fans cheered the hometown boy who had just shut up the Louisville Lip!

"Who's the prettiest *now?* Who's the prettiest *now?*" a group of white women shrieked at Muhammad, stamping their feet in delight.

Another man leaped into the ring screaming, "You finished, loudmouth! You finished!" From the audience someone else was shouting, "We beat you, you bastard. We got you! We got you!"

Others were screaming for Norton, who was suddenly a hero. Frazier had rushed up into the ring right after the fight to hug him. "I told you, I told you, didn't I?" Frazier shouted jubilantly. "I *knew* he could take Ali. Maybe now you can see how much I took out of Ali when I fought him, instead of how much he took out of me!"

Muhammad was pushing his way past policemen and crowds, trying to get to his dressing room. He was humiliated. This defeat was worse than his loss to Frazier. At least with the Frazier fight, there had been the possibility that Ali had actually outpointed his opponent.

But in this fight Muhammad had had his jaw *broken*. "There ain't no way to argue a broken jaw," he angrily thought to himself.

Muhammad was angriest with himself. He had taken Norton too lightly. He hadn't trained hard enough. He had thought that because he had won so many fights before the Norton bout, he would automatically win this one too. He was furious.

Inside the dressing room Muhammad's doctors were insisting that he be taken to the hospital immediately. But Muhammad had just been informed that his wife Belinda had gone into a state of shock after his loss to Norton. She was in another room down the hall in a state of hysteria, thinking Muhammad was dead!

Muhammad suddenly rushed back out of the room and down the hall to the room where Belinda was lying — strapped to a table.

"Pretty girl, pretty girl! I ain't dead," he said softly, leaning over his wife. "I ain't been beaten. I've been chastised. Allah give me a little punishment for not obeying the rules. I didn't train right. I didn't rest. I played all night."

"Don't worry, pretty girl," he continued soothingly. "Muhammad Ali is not dead, and nobody will ever kill me."

The following day, however, the press was declaring that Muhammad Ali was indeed dead — at least as far as his boxing career went.

"Muhammad Ali's career is finished," his old friend Howard Cosell proclaimed. "There is no rationale for Ali ever climbing into the ring again."

The people who still hated Muhammad Ali were also certain that he was finished. "The butterfly has lost its wings, the bee has lost its sting," said one hate letter sent to Muhammad, written on the back of a brown paper bag.

"You are through, you loudmouthed braggart," the letter continued. "Your mouth has been shut up for all times. It's a great day for America. You are finished."

Muhammad kept the letter. He especially liked the little poem: "The butterfly has lost its wings, the bee has lost its sting." Sometimes the people who hated Muhammad the most inspired him the most. As long as he knew those kinds of people were still around, he would have something to fight — he would still be fighting hatred and ignorance. Did people really think he was finished?

He intended to keep fighting, more determined than ever to recapture the heavyweight crown, now worn by George Foreman. First, however, Muhammad planned to settle the old scores.

He signed to fight a return bout with Ken Norton in September, 1973, six months after their match. Muhammad spent those six months in rigorous training, resolved to be in shape. He had built a training camp in the wooded area of Deer Lake, Pennsylvania, away from the distraction of city crowds and noise. Here he could train undisturbed.

Muhammad, at his training camp in Deer Lake, Pennsylvania, shows off his "superstrength."

Muhammad's efforts paid off. On September 10, he met Ken Norton a second time in the ring, and won the fight by the judges' decision. The public was astounded. Against all the odds, Muhammad Ali was making a second comeback!

Joe Frazier was next. He was Muhammad's old sore spot. Now that Frazier was no longer heavyweight champion, he was not so reluctant to fight Muhammad. They signed for

Muhammad punches the speed bag to help develop timing and coordination.

AFTER THE FALL, THE RISE 153

a match to be held in January, 1974. It was to be the battle of the losers — two former heavyweight champions still at war to determine who was the better fighter. Somehow, it seemed as if the battle would also determine who was the better man.

Over one billion people around the world viewed the second Muhammad Ali–Joe Frazier fight on January 28. It was called Superfight II, and brought in over eight million dollars — a figure unheard-of for a nonchampionship fight! Clearly these two "losers" represented more than two defeated gladiators clashing once again in the boxing arena. They had both risen above the sport, each representing certain values and truths to his respective following.

The values and truths embodied by Muhammad Ali won on that night of January 28. Muhammad went the entire twelve rounds with Joe Frazier and was declared the winner in a unanimous judges' decision. He was back again! Still a force to be reckoned with, Muhammad was now willing to settle for no less than the heavyweight crown, and he began demanding a fight with George Foreman.

Promoters smelled the scent of another superfight — an extravaganza which this time could surpass even the first two Muhammad Ali–Joe Frazier fights. It would be the fight of a lifetime — the final showdown for Muhammad Ali in a battle against George Foreman for the heavyweight championship!

Once again, the hype began grinding out. There was

Muhammad, flanked by Angelo Dundee, his trainer, and Drew Bundini Brown, his cornerman and sidekick, cools it in the ring.

talk of holding the fight in Africa. There was talk of a ten-million-dollar purse. And talking loudest was Muhammad Ali — already working his Black magic juju, doing his war dance, raising his spear, and gazing toward Africa, ready to rumble.

10
The Rumble in the Jungle

Float like a butterfly,
Sting like a bee.
Rumble young man, rumble
W-a-a-a-a-a-a-a-a!
— *Bundini Brown*

Sounds of Aretha Franklin belting out "Precious Lord" drifted from the loudspeakers, attached to the outdoor boxing ring in Zaire that was serving as a training area for both Muhammad Ali and George Foreman. Just a few minutes before, while Muhammad was training, the loudspeakers had been blaring out the throbbing rhythms of African drum music: *Boom-a-boom-a-boom-a-boom-a-boom-a-boom!*

But now it was George Foreman's turn to use the gym, and the sounds from the loudspeakers filled the sunlit African air with soulful, righteous gospel rock: "Precious Lord, take my hand. . . . Lead me on, let me staaaaand!" This was Foreman's training music: mellow, muted blues that had their roots in African rhythms.

Bundini was standing at the window of Muhammad's

apartment across the street from the gym, watching Foreman and his crew go in.

"So, how does Foreman look?" Muhammad asked. He was stretched out on a rubbing table being massaged.

"He's flabby," Bundini said, sounding pleased. "He's fat like a pregnant lady. If you fought him tonight, you'd kill him!"

Muhammad knew he was lucky to be fighting Foreman at all. It had taken months of haggling and wrangling with the twenty-five-year-old champion to get him to agree to put his crown on the line in a championship fight against Muhammad. Foreman, like Frazier before him, was enjoying his champion status. He knew that Muhammad was still the most popular fighter in the world, and didn't want to risk losing his crown in a fight which would bring out tremendous public support on the side of Muhammad.

But, like Frazier, Foreman also knew that until he fought and defeated Muhammad Ali, no one would regard him as the true champion. Muhammad's rematch fights with Joe Frazier and Ken Norton had established him once again as the most powerful force in boxing. That old Black magic was back, and he was demanding a confrontation with George Foreman to determine the real champion.

On the night he defeated Joe Frazier, Muhammad ran to the middle of the ring, grabbed the microphone and shouted into the Madison Square Garden audience: "Where's George? Where's George Foreman? You can tell George Foreman I'm ready for him!"

Promoters were also ready for a George Foreman–

Muhammad Ali championship match. It would possibly be the most exciting sports extravaganza in world history, surpassing even the Olympics. It could be worth literally *billions* of dollars.

Foreman, however, was still being stubborn. He had already turned down three offers for a match with Ali. It would finally take a Black promoter with the promise of a five-million-dollar purse to get the two fighters to agree to a match. And the fight arena would be in Africa itself — ancestral home of the world's Black people, a most fitting testing ground.

The promoter's name was Don King, and he was to the world of boxing promotion what Muhammad Ali was to the boxing game — a flashy, flamboyant huckster who combined an outrageous gift of gab with enormous confidence and the cunning to make possible the impossible.

King had come out of Cleveland, Ohio, where he spent his early days in the gambling and numbers racket. He had also spent four years in prison, convicted of killing a man in a fistfight. One look at King . . . it wasn't hard to imagine how he might have done such a thing. He was a massive man who towered over six feet, three inches. He sported a huge Afro that was always standing straight up, as if he had just been terribly frightened.

But Don King was afraid of nothing. Three years after seeing the first Muhammad Ali–Joe Frazier fight in 1971 from his prison cell, King had managed to wheel and deal his way to the top in fight promotion. He was the first Black to play a major role behind the scenes of boxing, where the deals are made and the real power lies. In two brief years, King raised more money for the sport of boxing than any other promoter in boxing history. In 1974, he set about becoming the prime architect for the George Foreman–Muhammad Ali match — a match other promoters had thought would never come off because of Foreman's reluctance.

But King went to George with an offer that finally even he couldn't refuse.

In a masterful stroke of promotional genius, King obtained a commitment of ten million dollars from the country of Zaire in Africa to sponsor the Foreman-Ali fight. It was the first time a *country* had ever offered to sponsor a fight, and it would be the first time a boxing match was held on African soil.

The upshot was that King could guarantee Foreman and Muhammad a purse of five million dollars each for the fight. *Five million dollars* for participation in a single event! It was staggering!

Even so, George Foreman was still wary. He wanted more money than Muhammad, for one thing. He wanted to be paid like a champion, which to him meant getting a larger purse than the challenger. Don King had to talk long and hard to convince him otherwise.

The promoter had tracked Foreman down in a Los Angeles parking lot to present the deal. "My dear man," King began in exasperation, "there is no other person you could fight that would bring in a purse of *one* million dollars, let alone five million. Now, let's be reasonable. You know that until you fight Ali there will always be a question as to who the real champion is."

That struck a nerve with Foreman. Although he now wore the crown, Foreman knew many people still considered Muhammad their champion.

"Look," King went on soothingly. "Everyone considers you a young Sonny Liston. Ali won't stand a chance against you. He's on his last legs and knows it. He just wants this one last fight before he retires."

Foreman was listening. Just a few weeks before, he had spoken to Muhammad, who had challenged him over the phone to a fight. The words from that conversation still rang in his ears.

"George!" Muhammad had shouted. "You think you got the nerve to get in the ring with me?"

"Anywhere, anytime, for the money!" Foreman fired back.

"They're talking about a purse of ten million dollars," Muhammad screamed. "Don King's coming out to see you with the contract. Sign it! And let's get it on, if you're not scared!"

"Scared of you, man? I just hope I don't kill you!" Foreman said, his voice trailing off.

Now, here was Don King standing before him, with the contract. *Five million dollars . . . You can't lose. . . . You're the young Sonny Liston, even bigger and better than he was. . . . Show 'em who the real champ is . . . !*

Foreman took the contract, stared at it for a long while, then finally signed. "If I find you've lied to me in any way, I'm backing out!" he said, glaring at King.

"*Lied* to you? My dear man, what do you take me for?" King said indignantly, snatching the contract once it was signed. "This is going to be the *event* of the century! Surely, even you must realize the enormous magnitude of the occasion in which you are about to participate. After centuries of separation, you and Ali — two prodigal sons — are returning to Africa, the land of your heritage, to stand symbolically in the sun. Two Black gladiators returning home!" Running the back of his diamond-studded hand across his forehead, King finished his little speech to Foreman and let out a long sigh. His statements frequently seemed like exaggerated pronouncements, but in this case, for once he had not overstated the facts.

Boom-*boom!* . . . Boom-*boom!* . . . Boom-*boom!* came the sounds of the war drums, a deep, steady, pulsating rhythm that rose and echoed throughout the city of Kinshasa, capital of Zaire. In a few weeks two warriors were to meet here, two Black Americans returning to Mother Africa to do battle, to mix their blood with the red African earth. The drums were heralding their homecoming, and the people were preparing to make them welcome.

Boom-*boom!* Boom-*boom!* Boom-*boom!*

African craftsmen were quickly working to remodel the old 20th of May Stadium, named for the date Zaire received independence, and located just outside of Kinshasa, where the fight was to be held. More than 60,000 people were expected to fill the stadium on September 24, 1974, the scheduled fight date. At least 12,000 of them would be tourists from all over the world who were flying in to witness the event.

A few, who had already arrived and found most of the hotel rooms reserved, were seeking accommodations in private African homes. They were bargaining with round-faced, copper-skinned African women in the marketplace for a place to stay. They offered money to young, thin African men in khaki shorts who could tell them where they might find a room — *any* room.

Kinshasa was being invaded — by journalists, photographers, television crews, sports fans, celebrities, and assorted others, who descended on the city like a plague of locusts. But the African people didn't mind. There was a mood of celebration in the air as they opened their hearts and their country to these foreign guests. Zaire, a lush and fertile country, rich in diamonds and copper, served as a delighted host to the match. It was not only welcoming two returning sons, but it was able to show the world its own dazzling magnificence: its majestic palm trees waving in the brilliant African sun; its sparkling rivers and brooks curving through the red ground; its sleek, gleaming white modern buildings reflecting the glow of the sunlight; its music, songs, drumming, chants, and dancing feet.

Muhammad and his crew arrived in the city of Kinshasa on September 10, two weeks before the fight date. The

Foreman fight would be his roughest test, and he had spent months readying himself for it.

Weeks before the trip to Zaire, up in the seclusion of Deer Lake, Pennsylvania, where he had built a new training camp, Muhammad had begun his preparations. The new training camp was a vivid contrast to Muhammad's former camps, which had all been in, or near, big cities. He loved the bustle and sounds and people of the cities. It was from the cities that he drew his strength.

But as he grew older, Muhammad began to require the peace and solace of the country, where he could go to rest and reflect, letting the fresh sweetness of natural surroundings soothe and renew him. The training camp in Deer Lake was such a setting. Located about thirty miles outside of Reading, Pennsylvania, high in the mountains, it had the quiet charm of rustic simplicity. A large cabin type of house served as the main quarters for Muhammad and his family. It was surrounded by smaller log cabin bunkhouses for Muhammad's vast crew. Huge boulders dominated much of the campsite area, and painted on each rock in large letters was the name of a past boxing champion . . . Joe Louis . . . Rocky Marciano . . . Sonny Liston . . . Sugar Ray Robinson.

Muhammad's father, a talented artist, had painted the names on the boulders, and they loomed as nature's own Boxing Hall of Fame. The training camp was called "Fighter's Haven," and Muhammad invited other boxers to use the camp while he trained.

He spent two months training for his fight with George

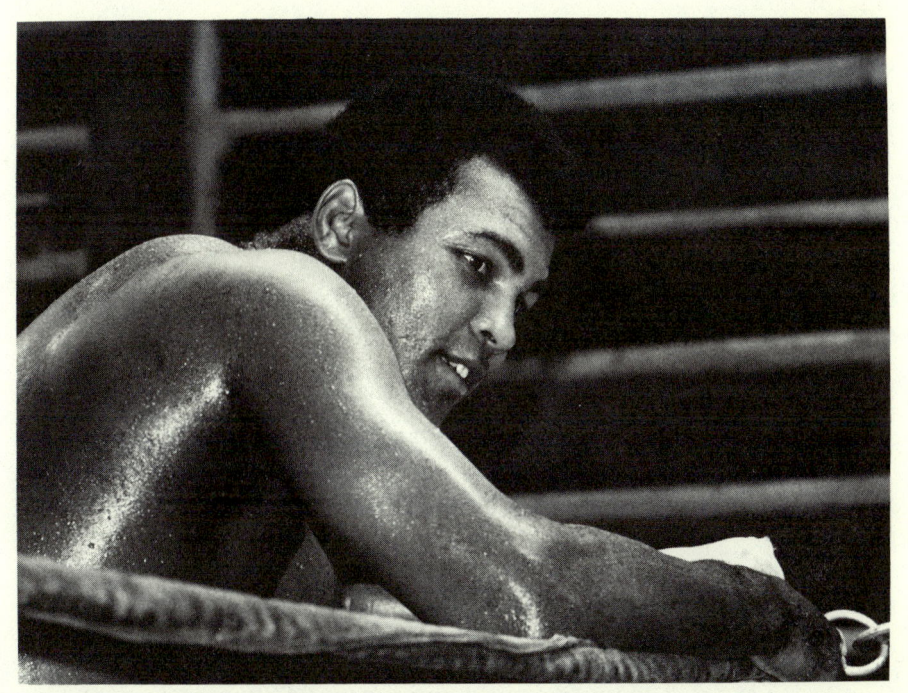

Taking a break, Muhammad relaxes on the ropes. (HELENE GAILLET)

Foreman. Before beginning actual training, Muhammad had first put his diet in order. That meant cutting out the ice cream and pies he loved so dearly, and eating only kosher foods prepared in a special way. (Black Muslims follow the same dietary laws as the Jewish people.)

Next, he began his roadwork. Muhammad always put in at least five days of running before he went into training in the gym. He would be up by dawn and out on the road, running through the woods, down the mountains, and along the highway. He forced himself to run until he felt he was almost ready to pass out. If he ran three miles and didn't feel tired, then he knew he had not worked hard enough. He would run for three more miles, pushing himself to the limit to build up stamina.

After five days of roadwork, Muhammad was ready to go into the gym to begin the real work of training. He first spent three rounds working out with the heavy bag — a five-foot-long, one-hundred-and-fifty-to-two-hundred-pound bag, which hung suspended from the ceiling by a thick rope. Muhammad would punch the heavy bag as if it were an opponent. But the bag was much more solid and rigid than a human being, and punching it helped to build up hitting power, and made the wrists and fists stronger.

Then he would work out on the speed bag, a smaller bag shaped like a beach ball, which snapped back the moment it was hit. Punching the speed bag helped to sharpen the eyes and build up the arms.

Next, Muhammad would jump rope. This exercise was very good for the wrists and leg muscles.

Finally, he would work out in the ring with his sparring partners. Muhammad always saved sparring until last during his training day. At the end of the day, when he was tired from roadwork and hitting the bags, his sparring partners would be fresh, forcing Muhammad to push even harder. Again, this was to build up stamina. Muhammad knew that during a real fight with George Foreman he would need plenty of stamina to go the full length of the fight without feeling tired.

After defeating Joe Frazier in his second fight with him, Muhammad had begun to talk frequently of retiring. He

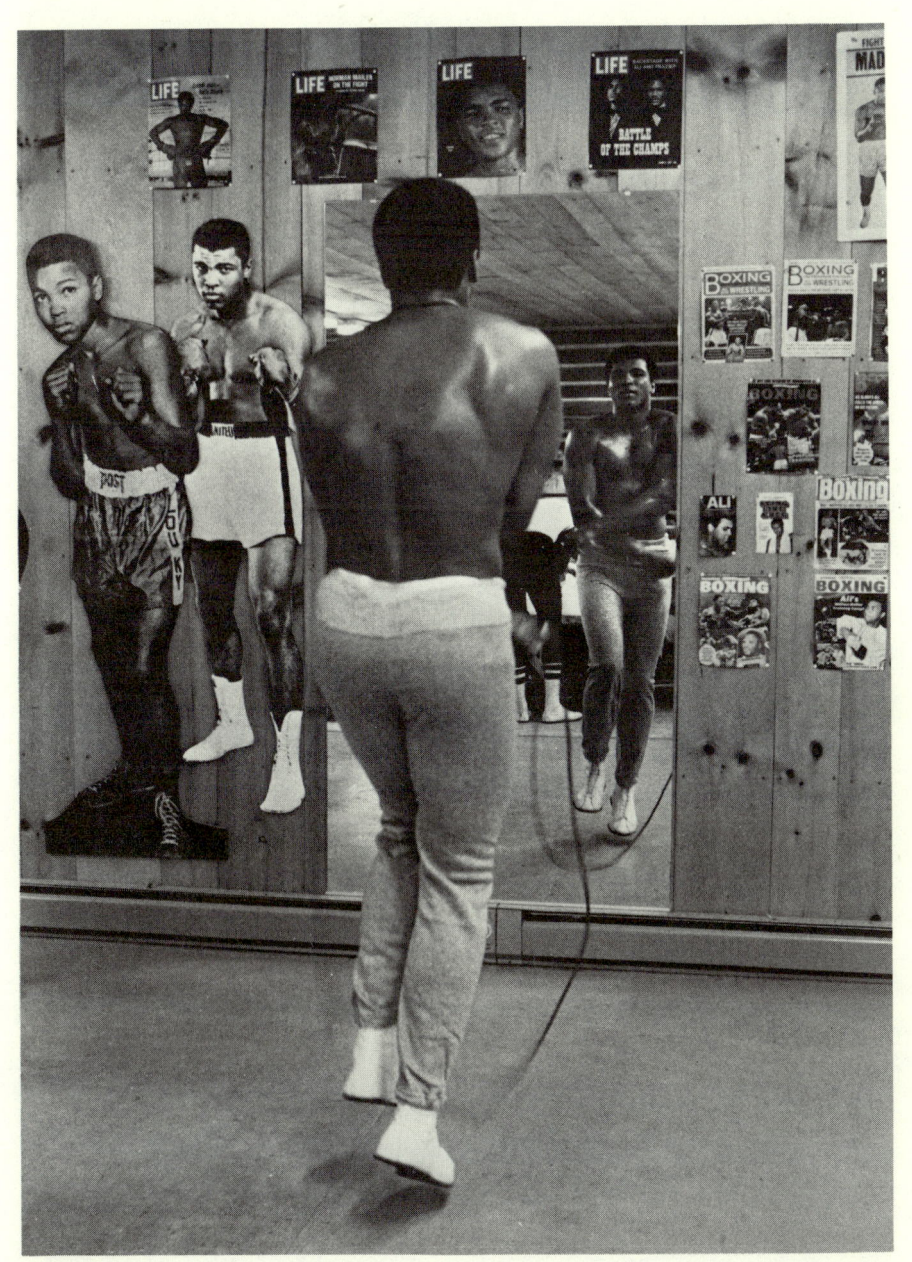

Muhammad, jumping rope, faces several images of himself — the one in the mirror and those on the wall (the picture nearest to Bundini is of Muhammad at twelve years old, when he first started boxing). (HELENE GAILLET)

wanted to spend more time with his wife, Belinda, and their four children — his oldest daughter, Maryum, his twin daughters, Jamillah and Rasheda, and his son, Muhammad, Jr. Muhammad realized that his boxing career was taking its toll on his family. He still recalled Belinda's agonized face that day he lost to Ken Norton, when she thought he had been killed. Yes, perhaps it was almost time to retire.

But Muhammad Ali wanted to leave the boxing game the way he had come in — a winner. Before he stepped down from the ring, he felt he had to show the world that he was still heavyweight champion. The fight with George Foreman would be his last chance to prove that, not only to the few people who still hated him, but to the millions of people who still loved him and believed in him. His victory would be their victory, too.

"When I see George Foreman in front of me, I think about Blacks being enslaved for three hundred years," Muhammad said, just before leaving for Zaire. "I think if he wins, we stay in chains."

"He's fighting the real champion," Muhammad continued emphatically, warming to the subject. "This will be the first time he feels like a challenger. He's not recognized yet until he comes through me! I'm gonna eat him up. I have wrestled with an alligator, tussled with a whale, handcuffed lightning, throwed thunder in jail . . . man, I'm *mean!*" he said, grinning.

But while Muhammad Ali may have been mean, George

The "Mouth" sounds off again at a press conference in Zaire, Africa, just before Muhammad's fight with George Foreman.

Foreman was considered even meaner, and was favored three to one to beat Muhammad in Zaire.

Foreman, standing in at six feet, three inches, weighed about 220 pounds, and was rated the strongest fighter in the history of boxing. He also had the highest knockout record — in 37 undefeated fights, he had won 34 of them by knockouts, and ten of the knockouts came within the first five minutes of the fight.

He was regarded as "the young Sonny Liston," and indeed, Foreman idolized Liston. Even his fighting style was similar to Liston's. And like Liston, Foreman was termed a "brute." His best punch was called an "anywhere punch" — one that wasn't aimed anywhere in particular but had the devastating power to break whatever it hit: a bone, a rib, a finger, anything.

"George is the first one I been in the ring with I know can kill you," recalled a former sparring partner of Foreman's. "He may never kill nobody, and I hope he never does, but he's got the power to kill, and he knows it."

Brought up on the ghetto streets of Houston, George Foreman had quit school in junior high. He and his friends stayed drunk on cheap wine, mugging and stealing whenever they felt like it to get money to buy more wine.

One day, while he was shooting pool in a local bar, Foreman saw two of his favorite athletes on television — football players Jim Brown and Johnny Unitas — doing a commercial for the Job Corps. The Job Corps was a free training program for young disadvantaged people, aimed at providing them with skills which would help them to earn their high school diplomas and then place them in good jobs.

Foreman, recognizing that he was headed for either jail or the grave if he continued leading his life of petty crime and boozing, decided to join the Job Corps. He was taken out of the squalid Houston ghetto and sent to the fresh, open-air Oregon climate to learn carpentry and bricklaying.

Proud of the new skills he learned in Oregon, Foreman next went to California to earn his high school diploma. It was there that he met Nick Broadus, a former lightweight fighter. Broadus was immediately impressed with Foreman's size and enormous strength. He started teaching him to box, and in 1968 George qualified for the Olympics in Mexico City. There he won the heavyweight Gold Medal in boxing, but in doing so, he also lost the respect and support of millions of Black people.

That summer the Olympics in Mexico City had been scandalized by the spectacle of two Black athletes raising their clenched fists in a defiant salute after winning medals in track. John Smith had won the Gold Medal and John Carlos had won the Bronze. Their fists were raised in militant protest against racist policies in America, the country for which both men had just won a medal.

It was a courageous act, but it cost the two men their medals. American Olympic officials were outraged and embarrassed by Smith and Carlos standing on the reviewing stands, with arms held high, and heads hung down as the "Star-Spangled Banner" played. How dare these two men ridicule America in front of millions of spectators!

On the other hand, George Foreman ran around the ring waving a tiny American flag after winning his Gold Medal. Officials were delighted. Now, this was the proper way for a Black athlete to act.

Other Blacks didn't think so. They were enraged. To them Foreman's act made a mockery of the brave actions taken by Smith and Carlos. To them George Foreman represented the supreme Uncle Tom — the white man's boy.

Thus, once again, in September, 1974, Muhammad Ali was set to battle a Great White Hope, who was considered to be the strongest fighter in boxing history.

Muhammad Ali was secretly a little worried about this fight with George Foreman. He knew George's reputation. He knew that George, at twenty-five, was much younger and fresher than he, now thirty-two. He knew he had lost much of his own speed. But he also knew that he could still outthink George. He knew that he could still come up with some surprise moves and strategies in the ring that would throw George off balance. He knew that George had never been defeated, and was therefore probably overconfident, cocky, underestimating his opponent. Muhammad knew the feeling. He had been there, and it had cost him a defeat to Ken Norton. He would make George Foreman pay the same price.

"What's he doing now?" Muhammad called to Bundini, who was still standing at the window of Muhammad's Kinshasa apartment watching Foreman in the gym across the street.

"He's sparring," Bundini answered; then he blurted out, "My God! How long is them rounds?"

"Foreman always spars for four-minute rounds and rests for half a minute in between," said one of Muhammad's sparring partners, who was also looking out the window. He had once sparred with Foreman, so he knew his habits. "Foreman's trainers work him like that to build up his stamina," he added.

"What else do he do when training?" Bundini demanded to know.

"Well, for one thing, during roadwork, Foreman runs *up* mountains," the fighter replied slowly.

"What you mean he runs *up* mountains? Can't nobody run *up* no mountains!" Bundini shouted, refusing to believe that George Foreman might really be a formidable opponent.

"It's true. I don't know how he does it. But he does. Runs up mountains."

"Good God!" Bundini said, looking back across the street at Foreman as if he were suddenly seeing him for the first time.

Muhammad jumped up from the rubbing table to come to the window to look, too. "Hmmmm," he said, sizing up the situation. "Most of them sparring partners he got working with him over there is just clowns. Just clowns." Then he turned and got back on the table.

As the time of the fight approached, spying between Muhammad's and Foreman's camps increased. Men would sit in on Muhammad's training sessions and then report back to Foreman, giving detailed descriptions of how Muhammad looked, whether or not he was in shape, what he seemed to be thinking, what his fighting strategy looked like. Of course, Muhammad's men were doing the same thing during Foreman's training sessions.

But just a few weeks before the fight, one of Muhammad's men returned to report some startling news. A sparring partner had cut Foreman's eye during a session. The fight would have to be postponed, and maybe even called off altogether!

Muhammad began to get that old sinking feeling he had often had while he was in exile — the feeling that came from having a fight dangled before him like a juicy plum and then abruptly snatched away.

"I shoulda known Foreman would try to back out of this fight at the last minute!" he said bitterly. "Well, I ain't gonna let him off that easy!"

Muhammad heard that Foreman and his trainer, Dick Sadler, were planning to fly out of Zaire to Paris, where George would rest and recuperate. Muhammad quickly called a press conference.

"That's right," he told the assembled reporters. "George and his trainer will be trying to sneak out of the country to keep from having to fight me. If I was the president of Zaire, I'd block all the airports to make sure they didn't get out. After all, this country's put up ten million dollars for this fight. And now it might all go down the drain just because George is running scared!"

Reporters were hurriedly taking notes, and a few hours later, they had contacted Foreman himself.

"Ali says you're trying to leave town 'cause you're scared," several reporters told him. "Is that true?"

Muhammad knew Foreman's pride would make him deny the charges. Foreman's pride also kept him in Zaire. He didn't want to appear to be afraid of Muhammad by flying to Paris.

Again, Muhammad had outsmarted his opponent even before getting him in the ring. Half of the battle had already been won.

The fight was rescheduled for October 30, a month later than the first date. It was to be held at four o'clock in the morning to avoid the blazing heat of the African sun. But the outdoor 20th of May Stadium was still going to be hot. The lights of television cameras from all over the world had been hooked up. Over 60,000 human bodies jammed together would generate even more heat. And the temperature in Zaire, even at dawn, was expected to be in the eighties. The conditions were less than ideal for any fight, but in this case, they only added to the drama.

The fight was being billed as simply that — The Fight. As one magazine editorial said: "Forget everything else, every fight that has been won or lost before, and all of those that will be contested in years to come. Forget every battle of man against man, of mind against mind, of soul against soul. This is the one. This is the greatest."

✳   ✳   ✳

October 30. Three in the morning. The countdown begins. In another hour Muhammad will be going out to face the toughest challenger and the toughest fight of his life. It has been ten years since he first stepped into the ring to take the heavyweight crown from Sonny Liston. He will now be attempting to regain the crown from Liston's "ghost," George Foreman.

As the clock moves toward four o'clock, Muhammad, waiting nervously in his dressing room, sees those ten years flash before him: the victories and the defeats, the successes and the setbacks. They have all made him stronger — ready for this last rite of passage.

Muhammad and his manager, Herbert Muhammad,

kneel, as they always do before a fight, and offer a prayer to Allah. Then they embrace, like two brothers who are about to embark on a journey, uncertain of where it will lead, but knowing they cannot turn back. They have already come too far.

"It's time! It's time!" someone shouts from outside the dressing room. "It's fight time!"

Muhammad gets up slowly from the rubbing table. Bundini puts Muhammad's new robe around him, with its ornate African designs embossed on the back, and they move toward the door. Muhammad hears the shouting coming from the stadium as soon as he opens the door.

"Aleeeee! Bomayeeeee!" ("Kill!") the crowd is roaring. Muhammad feels the old surge of strength which a cheering crowd always gives him.

He and his entourage begin their procession to the stadium. Leading the way are two men, one carrying an American flag and the other carrying the flag of Zaire.

As they approach the ramp leading to the stadium, Muhammad looks up and — silhouetted against the dusky African sky, blazing with the hot fire of television lights — he sees the people, 62,000 of them, mostly dark-skinned Africans, dressed in fiery colors of golden yellows, hot reds, earth browns, and oranges. As far as the eye can see, there are people, screaming wildly, frenzied, paying homage to the returning warrior, who is back to collect his due.

Aleeeee! Bomayeeeee! . . . Aleeeee! Bomayeeeee!

Boom-*boom!* Boom-*boom!* Boom-*boom!* comes the beat of the war drum. The warrior is *back!*

Muhammad gets into the ring, takes off his robe, and sweeps his hand through the air, acknowledging the people. They go wild. "Aleeeeeee!"

Foreman takes his time entering the stadium. He wants to make Muhammad wait. But Muhammad doesn't mind the waiting. He is being filled with the strength of the people. Each cheer is infusing him with new power.

At last, George Foreman makes his entrance. The people begin shouting for him. Foreman gets into the ring and moves to his corner to wait. "George Foreman! The Champion!" people shout.

Zack Clayton, the referee, calls the two men to the middle of the ring to give the final instructions. The two fighters move back to their corners to wait, conjuring up in their heads, for the last time, their own juju — their own Black magic.

And then the fight is *on!*

Round 1: Muhammad moves out and throws a fast left jab. He is dancing. But Foreman is cutting off the ring by taking large steps, which force Muhammad to keep moving. He is taking six steps for every two that Foreman takes.

"Come on, chump!" Muhammad suddenly cries. "Show me what you got. You been hitting kindergarten kids!"

Foreman corners Muhammad on the ropes and shoots out a left-handed "anywhere" punch, striking Muhammad

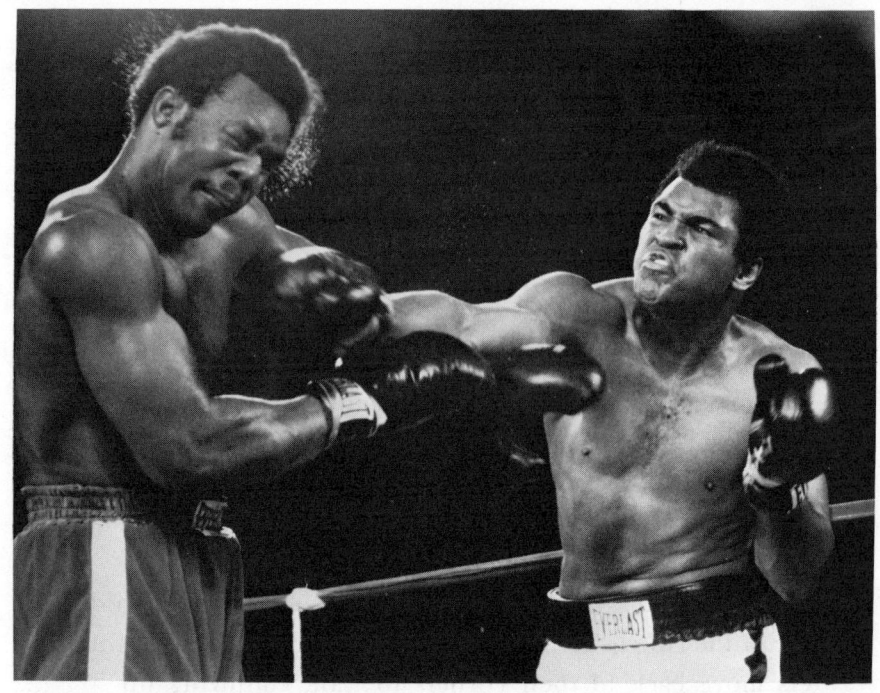

The sweat flies from Foreman as Muhammad lands a quick right to his jaw. (CAMERA 5, KEN REGAN)

with deadly power and accuracy. Muhammad's cornermen are screaming for him to move.

"Move, Champ! Get off the ropes!"

Muhammad had planned to stay off the ropes, but he can see that Foreman is continuing to cut the ring, making it impossible for Ali to dance without quickly getting tired.

Round 2: Muhammad again moves out quickly and starts shooting jabs. Foreman is still cutting the ring, and Muhammad knows he will have to change his strategy. He begins leaning against the ropes, forcing Foreman to come in after him. Muhammad realizes he is taking a chance fighting from the ropes, but it seems to him it's the only chance he has. Foreman is throwing punches that land with the force of bombs. He has the hitting power of Joe Louis and Rocky Marciano combined, and Muhammad has already felt that power.

Round 3: Muhammad comes out, shooting jabs that sting. But they only seem to stun Foreman briefly, who moves in on Muhammad like a tank. Again, Muhammad retreats to the ropes.

"All right, sucker! This is where you want me!" Muhammad calls to him. "Come on and get me!" Round three is the round in which Foreman's people have been predicting he will win.

Foreman moves in, throwing deadly punches at Muhammad's head. Then he reaches up with a swift uppercut that hits Muhammad's jaw. Ali feels as if his whole head were coming off.

Muhammad's people are enraged that he's lying against the ropes.

"Get off them ropes! Dance, Champ! Dance!" they scream. But Muhammad is paying no attention. His long-shot chance now is to make Foreman tired by getting him to punch *himself* out, as he tries to beat Muhammad to death.

During rounds four, five, six, and seven, Muhammad continues his rope strategy. He begins to feel Foreman slowing down, although he keeps coming on with brutal strength.

Near the end of round seven, Muhammad, in a clinch with Foreman, whispers in his ear: "You got eight more rounds to go, sucker! *Eight* more rounds, and look how tired you are. I ain't even got started, and you out of breath!" The bell sounds, ending the round.

Round 8: Foreman has gone into the eighth round of a fight only three times in his life. Now, he is feeling shaky. Some of the old confidence is beginning to slip. Muhammad's lying against the ropes and teasing are getting to him.

Foreman throws a long left punch, which Muhammad blocks by throwing a right cross punch. It connects.

The crowd begins screaming for Muhammad. "Ali! Ali! Bomaye! Kill him! Kill him!"

Muhammad knows it is now time to come out with everything he has — to play it to a bust. While Foreman is trying to recover from Muhammad's last punch, Muhammad reaches back, and with all the spirit and the power and the juju that is in him, he shoots a straight right punch to Foreman's jaw. He hears and feels the punch smash into Foreman's face. At first Foreman stands still, and then Muhammad sees the lights in Foreman's eyes begin to go out.

Foreman is falling . . . falling . . . doubled over in a jackknife position, he hits the floor.

The crowd is on its feet screaming. *Aleeeee!*

The referee is kneeling on the floor next to Foreman, doing the count, while Muhammad stands in a corner watching.

George Foreman goes down and stays down for the ten count, making Muhammad the new heavyweight champion.

(CAMERA 5, KEN REGAN)

"Six-seven-eight-nine-ten! He's *out!*" Clayton screams. Muhammad is already in the center of the ring, his arms waving in victory.

"The new world heavyweight champion . . . *Muhammad Aliii!*" Clayton shouts over the noise of the people, holding up Muhammad's arm.

"*Aleeeee! Aleeeee! Aleeeee! Aleeeee!*" the people shout. They dance and cry and hug each other, and then finally break through the guards to leap into the ring, still screaming in jubilation.

"*Aleeeeeee!*" The cry goes up all over the world . . . in New York, where crowds get roaring drunk in victory celebration . . . in Tokyo, where sedate Japanese businessmen and young schoolboys chant happily, A—leee! . . . in London . . . in Paris . . . all over the globe.

Muhammad Ali is the winner! Against all the odds and all the obstacles, he has come back to take his rightful place in the sun, to stand as the greatest, as the people's champion.

❊   ❊   ❊

Muhammad Ali did not retire after regaining the heavyweight crown, as he had so often talked of doing. Rather, he went on to fight Joe Frazier and Ken Norton again, to take on a Japanese wrestler in Tokyo, and to defend his crown several times against lesser opponents. Today he is still a man shrouded in controversy and contradictions. He is still a man who has his share of enemies.

But Muhammad Ali may also possibly be this century's greatest shining star — a star still rising, leaving behind it a legacy of inspiration and of hope. Because if Muhammad Ali is a winner, it means that truth and decency and integrity and justice are also winners.

792404

796.8 Edwards, Audrey
EDW
    Muhammad Ali: the
      people's champ

DATE			
11-13-80			
1-81			
5-28-81			
OCT 12 '81			
12-7-81			
JAN 7 '82			
MAR 17 '82			
APR 15 '82			

© THE BAKER & TAYLOR CO.